بِسْمِ اللّٰهِ الرَّحْمٰنِ الرَّحِيْمِ

"In the name of Allah the most affectionate, the most merciful"

THE
NEW MUSLIMS
HANDBOOK

D1664150

Author:
Mohammed J. Rahman

Table of Contents

Chapter 5: Salaah (Prayer) -.............................…....Page 58

Chapter 9: Seerah (Life of the Prophet Muhammad, peace be upon him) -…..……………………..…… Page 118

Introduction

The purpose of producing this book is to give new Muslims the confidence to build their knowledge of Islam. Although this work is titled "The New Muslims Handbook," the reader doesn't necessarily need to be a new Muslim. The contents covered in this book are somewhat basic and what every Muslim should know. This book will be useful to Muslims who may have lost interest in the religion and may be seeking a tool to come back to Islam. Or, this book can certainly be used by those interested in Islam, as it will cover a wide variety of topics with clarity by using evidence from the Quran, the life of the Prophet, peace be upon him, and notable scholars of earlier generations.

The book will cover the fundamentals of Islam, such as: What is Islam? What does it mean to be a Muslim? The first part of the book will predominantly consist of the 5 pillars of Islam, as these are the groundings of any Muslim. What faith actually means as well as tenants of faith will be covered in the first. This will then be followed by the manners and etiquette that Muslims should have. Before seeking any sort of knowledge, there is a system that the seeker should abide by in order to maximise their learning. Therefore, this chapter has been placed after understanding what faith truly is and before we go deeper into the 5 pillars of Islam.

An important note to mention here is that the book will mainly consist of Hanafi law. The reasoning for this is that I am a Hanafi myself, but the majority of the Muslim world also follows the Hanafi school of thought. In Part 2 of this book, we will cover why a school of thought (the school of fiqh) must be followed. It's consequences of not obeying the school of fiqh and the history of the 4 Imams of Jurisprudence.

I have tried to lay out this book in a sequential pattern to make it easier for the reader to understand. For example, without purification, worship cannot take place. Therefore, the chapter of purification has come before the chapter of prayer, as purification must be done prior to engaging in Salaah. When it comes to verses of the Quran, the translation has been mainly taken from the "Kanzul-Imaan" of Imam Ahmad Raza Khan. Some wordings have been changed by the editors of this book, as they are qualified imams and Islamic judges (Mufti's).

Chapter 1- What is Islam?:
This chapter lays the foundation by defining Islam, exploring its etymology, core beliefs (the Shahada), and the Five Pillars of Islam. It delves into the significance of Tawhid (the oneness of God), Prophethood, and the Quran as the holy book.

Chapter 2- Faith:
Explore the nuances of faith in Islam, encompassing articles of faith such as belief in angels, divine books, predestination (qadar), and the day of Judgement (Akhirah). This chapter emphasises the importance of sincere belief and its impact on a Muslim's life.

Chapter 3 - Manners and Etiquette for a Muslim:
Detailing ethics and etiquette, this chapter covers topics such as kindness, respect, honesty, patience, and generosity, highlighting their importance in daily interactions and societal conduct.

Chapter 4- Purification:
Its rules and regulations. A comprehensive guide to ritual purification (Tahara) encompassing ablution (Wudu), Ghusl (ritual bathing), and Tayammum (dry ablution). It covers the spiritual significance and practical aspects of purification in Islam. Rulings related to women will also be covered in this section.

Chapter 5 - Salaah (prayer) :
Laws and methods of prayer a step-by-step explanation of Salaah (prayer), including its timings, postures, and supplications. It provides detailed instructions on how to perform the five daily prayers and their significance in a Muslim's life.

Chapter 6 - Fasting:
Beyond Ramadan, this chapter explores voluntary fasting, the spiritual benefits of fasting, and the etiquettes observed during this blessed month.

Chapter 7 - Zakaat:
Understanding the obligation of Zakaat (charitable giving) in Islam, its calculation, and the impact it has on societal welfare. It also discusses Sadaqah (voluntary charity) and its virtues.

Chapter 8 - Hajj:
A comprehensive guide to the pilgrimage, Hajj, detailing its rituals, historical significance, and spiritual journey. It includes practical advice for those intending to perform hajj.

Chapter 9 - The Seerah of the Prophet Muhammad (peace be upon him):
A brief exploration of the life, teachings, and character of Prophet Muhammad (peace be upon him), highlighting his role as the final messenger and his exemplary conduct.

Chapter 10 - Biographies of the Four Caliphs:
Dive into the lives of Hazrat Abu Bakr, Hazrat Umar, Hazrat Uthman, and Hazrat Ali (may Allah continue to raise their ranks), understanding their contributions and leadership in the early Islamic period.

Chapter 11 - Short Biographies of the Four Imams:
Exploring the lives and teachings of Imam Abu Hanifa, Imam Malik, Imam Shafi'i, and Imam Ahmad bin Hanbal, discussing the importance of following a school of thought (Madhab).

Chapter 12 - Spiritual Refinement:
A guide to self-improvement and spiritual growth, focusing on developing virtues, inner peace, and strengthening one's connection with Allah. This chapter will highlight renowned spiritual masters in Islamic history. As well as contemporary spiritual leaders.

Chapter 13 - The End of Times, Resurrection, and Judgement Day:
Reflecting on Islamic beliefs regarding the signs of the Day of Judgement, resurrection, accountability, and the ultimate fate of humanity.

Chapter 14 - General Q&A:
Addressing common questions and misconceptions about Islam, providing clear and concise explanations.

Chapter 15 - Short Surahs with Translation and Transliteration, and Duas (supplications):
Compilation of selected short chapters from the Quran with translations, transliterations, and essential supplications for various occasions.

The book will then end with closing statements by the author.

Chapter 1

What is Islam?

Islam means submission to God. Islam is an endless ocean of knowledge; hence, the idea came about to compile this book to give the reader an outline of the basics of Islam. The foundation of Islam is to believe that there is one God and that the Prophet Muhammad, peace be upon him, is his final messenger.

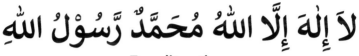

لاَ إِلٰهَ إِلَّا اللهُ مُحَمَّدٌ رَّسُوْلُ اللهِ

Transliteration:
Laa-Ila-aha-Il-lall-ahu-mu-ham-madur-rasool-ullah

Translation:
"There is no God worthy of worship except Allah and Muhammad is His messenger"

Muslims must believe in all the names and attributes of Allah.

Islam is a religion of peace; it sets out guidelines like no other religion. Islam has authentic sources of knowledge that have been passed down from the time of the prophet Muhammad, peace be upon him, until now, through the preservation of the Quran and the transmission of Hadith (sayings and teachings of the Prophet, peace be upon him) from reliable scholars. For example, his students (companions) and his family of the Prophet Muhammad (peace be upon him) transmitted what they heard, observed, and learned to those after them, and their students did the same, with this tradition continuing in every generation until the knowledge reached us today. Islam is the only religion with a systematic transmission that no other religion has.

To fully understand the Quran, one must look into the life of the Prophet, peace be upon him, as he is the walking Quran and is the best exemplar of the teachings of the Quran. How the Prophet peace be upon him lived, socialised, his working life as a tradesman, and any other aspect of a person's life you look at, Islam has the answer to it through the transmission of Hadith. This is where famous Hadith books, such as Bukhari, Muslim, and many others, come into play. No other religion has this process; rather, they have the possibility of going straight to their holy text and having a chance of misinterpreting the words to possibly suit their own desires. This is exactly what has happened to Christianity since the time of Jesus (Prophet Isa). Peace be upon him. Bishops and other heads have misinterpreted and changed the Bible for centuries, to the extent that the Bible isn't what was revealed to Jesus (Isa). Peace be upon him.

A beauty of Islam is that it is part of faith to believe in all prophets. Which other religion teaches compassion and love towards all prophets?

Which other religion offers more extensive knowledge in cosmology, biology, and many other sciences than Islam? 1,400 years ago, the Quran was revealed over a span of 23 years. The revelation covers how the Lord's creation began, how embryology works, cosmology, how the seas meet, and much more. Islam is a beautiful religion that gives you a sense of guidance and understanding. It has the answers to all the issues that are going on in the world.

Islam has laws for every aspect of life, from purification to how to eat, how to bathe, how to socialise, and beyond. It is not a religion where you can pick and choose what you want to believe in.

The pillars of Islam are 5:

1. Faith: belief that there is no god except Allah and that Muhammad, peace be upon him, is his final messenger.

2. Salah (prayer): to observe the five daily prayers.

3. Ramadan: to fast in the month of Ramadan.

4. Zakaat: to give alms of 2.5% of your wealth every year to the poor.

5. Hajj: To make the pilgrimage to Makkah at least once in your lifetime.

This is what it means to be a Muslim. Many Muslims struggle with the basics of praying five times a day, but it is important to bear in mind that it is the first thing for which they will be accountable on the day of judgment.

عَنْ أَبِي هُرَيْرَةَ قَالَ قَالَ رَسُولُ اللَّهِ صَلَّى اللَّهُ عَلَيْهِ وَسَلَّمَ إِنَّ
أَوَّلَ مَا يُحَاسَبُ بِهِ الْعَبْدُ يَوْمَ الْقِيَامَةِ مِنْ عَمَلِهِ صَلَاتُهُ فَإِنْ
صَلُحَتْ فَقَدْ أَفْلَحَ وَأَنْجَحَ وَإِنْ فَسَدَتْ فَقَدْ خَابَ وَخَسِرَ
فَإِنْ انْتَقَصَ مِنْ فَرِيضَتِهِ شَيْءٌ قَالَ الرَّبُّ عَزَّ وَجَلَّ انْظُرُوا
هَلْ لِعَبْدِي مِنْ تَطَوُّعٍ فَيُكَمَّلَ بِهَا مَا انْتَقَصَ مِنْ الْفَرِيضَةِ ثُمَّ
يَكُونُ سَائِرُ عَمَلِهِ عَلَى ذَلِكَ سنن الترمذي كتاب الصلاة
باب ما جاء أن أول ما يحاسب به العبد يوم القيامة

Translation: Abu Huraira reported: The Messenger of Allah, peace and blessings be upon him, said, "The first action for which a servant of Allah will be held accountable on the Day of Resurrection will be his prayers. If they are in order, he will have prospered and succeeded. If they are lacking, he will have failed and lost. If there is something defective in his obligatory prayers, then the Almighty Lord will say: See if My servant has any voluntary prayers that can complete what is insufficient in his obligatory prayers. The rest of his deeds will be judged the same way." Sunan al Tirmidhi 413

Chapter 2

Faith

Kalima Tayyib

The ultimate testimony of faith is:

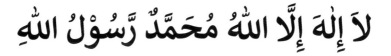

Transliteration:
Laa-ilaa-ha-ill-al-laa-hu-mu-ham-ma-dur-rasool-ullah

Translation:
"There is no God worthy of worship except Allah and Muhammad is his messenger."

This is known as "Kalima" in Arabic, which translates into English as "phrase." There are six kalima's that the Muslim should know and memorise. This first Kalima is called "Kalima Tayyib" or "Kalima Tayyibah," meaning "Pure Phrase.".

As long as one believes this statement in their hearts, then they are a Muslim. It is no good to say this with the tongue alone when you do not believe this firmly deep down inside you. As a Muslim, you must believe that Muhammad, peace be upon him, is the final messenger of Allah. Every religion believes in a God, but what classifies them as non-Muslims is that they do not have faith in Muhammad. Peace be upon him as the seal of all prophets. How much of a beautiful and powerful name is Muhammad, peace be upon him? It is that name that determines whether you are a Muslim or not. Subhan-Allah, this is the status of our final prophet, and it will always continue to rise, for Allah says:

"And We raise your reputation high."
(Surah Al-Inshirah, Chapter 94 : Verse 4)

Kalima Shahadah

The second Kalima is known as "Shahadah" which means "Testify"

أَشْهَدُ أَنْ لَّا إِلهَ إِلَّا اللهُ وَحْدَهُ لَا شَرِيْكَ
لَهُ وَأَشْهَدُ أَنَّ مُحَمَّدًا عَبْدُهُ وَرَسُوْلُهُ

Transliteration:
Ash-hadu-al-laa-ilaa-ha-ill-al-laa-hu-wah-dahu-laa-sharee-
ka-lahu-wa-ash-hadu- anna-mu-hamm-madan-ab-duhu-wa-
ra-soo-luhu

Translation:
*"I bear witness that there is no God except Allah, He is alone,
He has no partners. And I bear witness that Muhammad is
His servant and messenger."*

Kalima Tawheed

لَا إِلهَ إِلاَّ أَنْتَ وَاحِدًا لاَّ ثَانِي لَكَ مُحَمَّدٌ
رَّسُوْلُ اللهِ إِمَامُ الْمُتَّقِيْنَ رَسُوْلُ رَبِّ
الْعَالَمِيْنَ

Transliteration:
Laa-ila-ha-il-laa-anta-waa-hi-dal-laa-thaa-niya-laka-mu-
ham-madur-rasool-ul-laahi-imaa-mul-mut taqee-na-rasoolu-
rab-bil-a-la-meen

Translation:

"There is no God except you, You are One who has no second. Muhammad is the Messenger of God, the Leader of the Pious and the Messenger of the Lord of the Universe."

Kalima Tamjeed

لَا إِلٰهَ إِلَّا أَنْتَ نُوْرًا يَّهْدِيَ اللهُ لِنُوْرِهِ مَنْ يَّشَآءُ مُحَمَّدٌ رَّسُوْلُ اللهِ إِمَامُ الْمُرْسَلِيْنَ خَاتَمُ النَّبِيِّيْنَ

Transliteration:

Laa-ilaa-ha-il-laa-an-ta-noo-ray-yah-diya-al-laa-hu-li-noo-ri-hi-mai-ya-shaa-u mu-ham-madur-ra-sool-ul-laahi-imaa-mul-mur-saleena-khaa-tamun-nabiy-yeen

Translation:

"There is no God except you, A Light who guides with His light whom He wills. Muhammad is the Messenger of God, the Leader of the Messengers and the Seal of the Prophets."

Imaan-E-Mujmal (Summary of declaration of faith)

اٰمَنْتُ بِاللهِ كَمَا هُوَ بِاَسْمَآئِهِ وَصِفَاتِهِ وَقَبِلْتُ جَمِيْعَ اَحْكَامِهِ وَاَرْكَانِهِ

Transliteration:

Aa-man-thu-bil-laa-hi-ka-ma-huwa-bi-asmaa-i-hee-wa-si-faathi-hi-wa-qa-bil-thu-ja-mee-a-ah-kaa-mihi-wa-ar-kaa-ni-hee

Translation:

I have faith in Allah as he is known by his names and attributes and I accept all his commands

Imaan-E-Mufassal (Detailed declaration of faith)

اٰمَنْتُ بِاللهِ وَمَلٰئِكَتِهِ وَكُتُبِهِ وَرُسُلِهِ وَالْيَوْمِ الْاٰخِرِ وَالْقَدْرِ خَيْرِهِ وَشَرِّهِ مِنَ اللهِ تَعَالٰى وَالْبَعْثِ بَعْدَ الْمَوْتِ

Transliteration:

Aa-man-thu-bil-lahi-wa-malaa-ika-thi-hi-wa-kuthu-bihi-wa-ru-su-lihi-wal-yaw-mil akhiri-wal-qadri-khai-ri-hi-wa-shar-rihi-min-alla-hi-ta-aala-wal-ba-thi-ba-dal-mawth

Translation:

"I have faith in Allah and his angels and his books and his messengers, and the day of judgement and that all good and evil and fate is from almighty Allah and it is sure that there will be resurrection after death."

To be a Muslim, one must believe in the above testimonies, as these are the pillars of faith for a Muslim. A Muslim cannot have any doubts about the testimony of faith, as this will weaken their faith. The more knowledge you gain of Allah, the more one will understand the tenants of faith and their importance.

Chapter 3

Manners & etiquettes of a Muslim

A Muslim should always display good manners and etiquette. This is easier said than done. However, with the right companionship and guidance from a teacher or mentor, this can be improved over time. It's extremely easy for people in general to lose their manners and etiquette. This could be due to anger, having a stressful day at work, or possibly dealing with family problems and many other issues. It is no good for a Muslim to engage in worship while being cruel or rude to others. We see many people pray five times a day but still have the habit of lying, deceiving others, and so forth. As a Muslim, you must follow Islam wholeheartedly, not pick and choose whatever best suits you.

I have included some sayings of the Prophet peace be upon him regarding manners and etiquettes. I hope the reader will be able to capture the importance of this topic in Islam.

"Nothing is heavier on the scale of deed than one's good manners" (Bukhari)

"The most beloved of Allah's slaves to Allah are those with the best manners." (At-Tabrani)

"A person may attain through good manners the same level of virtue as those who spend their nights in prayer." (Saheeh Al-Bukhari)

'The best among you in Islam are those with the best manners," (Saheeh Bukhari)

When asked about the definition of righteousness, the Prophet (peace be upon him) replied, "Righteousness is good character," (Saheeh Bukhari)

"Modesty only causes good," (Saheeh Bukhari)

The reason why this chapter has been placed after faith is because Imaan (faith) is the basis, and before seeking knowledge, one must be well mannered. You cannot be an arrogant seeker of knowledge, as knowledge is supposed to humble an individual and make them realise that they are nothing but a drop in the ocean. Knowledge takes you to Allah and to the Prophet, peace be upon him. Knowledge can also take one to the depths of hellfire. Why? It is solely based on intention and how much one has acted upon what they have learned. Manners and etiquette are a branch of faith for a Muslim; without the branches, the tree is not complete. The tree may look deformed or unattractive. Similarly, a Muslim who lacks manners and etiquette will be unpleasing to those around him or her.

When conveying the message of peace (giving a fellow Muslim Salaam), make sure the recipient isn't occupied in another conversation, whether it's in person or on the phone. This may make it difficult for them to respond. It is Sunnah (practice of the Prophet, peace be upon him) to convey the Salaam first, but it is mandatory for the recipient to respond. Therefore, if it is not feasible for a person to respond, do not burden them with the salam. This also applies to whether a person is eating, regardless of whether they're alone or in a group. How do you expect one to respond to a Salaam when food is in their mouth? When eating, a person should take their time and eat slowly. It is against the Sunnah to eat in a rapid motion. When someone is eating and you give them Salaam, they may feel the need to chew their food quickly, which may cause choking or something else of a similar nature. Therefore, in this situation, it is better not to give Salaam to a fellow Muslim. The message of peace should also be conveyed in a peaceful manner. With a soft, gentle tone. Not a harsh, arrogant tone. Salaam of such nature is void, and you're better off not giving Salaam with a negative attitude. If you see one in a rush, it is better not to stop them from conversing, as they may have somewhere important to attend or maybe be running late for something. It is not necessary to engage in conversation with them in that state unless both parties are willing to.

When shaking hands with fellow Muslims (with the same gender only, of course), make sure nothing is in your hand. The prophetic method of shaking hands is to use both hands and not just one hand.

Manners of speech are something many of us lack. It is part of Adaab (manners/etiquettes). When speaking, make sure your speech is clear and precise. Be straight to the point so those you're communicating with may understand you. Do not speak in a harsh-paced tone where people will find it difficult to understand you. This is part of the Sunnah of the prophet, peace be upon him. To be spiritually uplifted, one must always try to be conscious of the presence of Allah (God). This leads to my next point of abundance speech. Many of us get lost in useless speech. Such as talking about sports for hours and hours on end, or the latest celebrity rumour, and so forth. In the real world, we all have some sort of attachment to a celebrity. But we must always remember that gossip about these individuals will not bring us much spiritual benefit. There is no harm in looking up to a role model. For example, many people adore the legendary boxer Muhammad Ali. Why? Not only for his in-ring performance, but many of us remember him for what he did for humanity. One may be inspired by a wealthy individual because they may want to attain that level of wealth, for which there is no harm in Islam as long as it's a Halal (lawful) way of earning income. But it does not mean we should dedicate our conversations to these people at all times. The prophet peace be upon him said, "Do not talk too much without remembrance of Allah. Indeed, excessive talking without remembrance of Allah hardens the heart. And indeed, the furthest of people from Allah is the harsh-hearted." (Sunan al-Tirmidhi 2411). As humans, we may fall into error and backbite or slander individuals. We must try to refrain from this, and if we are victims of this, we should seek forgiveness from Allah and have the intention to not do the sin again. Being conscious of speech will slowly lead to being conscious of Allah (God). Next time, when you may want to talk about someone behind their back, you will be fearful of Allah and that the Lord is all seeing and all hearing. Try your best to refrain from arguments and debates. It has no benefit and has more of a possibility of leading to greater troubles. Especially with debates. How many debates have we seen where one party admits their mistake or fault? Extremely little. If anything, it proves to one's ego that they were right in the first place. The smart Muslim will always try to be better than yesterday; these issues can cause the soul to tarnish. Therefore, one should try to avoid debates and arguments. If there's something you do not agree with, Then, in a polite manner, your opinion should be addressed.

If there are three of you, two of the three should not engage in their own conversation or speak in a language that the third person does not understand. This can make them feel isolated and may cause distress. Two of the three should not whisper to each other or leave the third person out of the conversation.

When entering a person's house, the visitor should wait for the host to invite them in, even if it's family. The host may be tidying up the house, making space for the guest, or maybe engaged in something important. Therefore, the visitor should wait outside until the host invites them in. It is the manners of the host to ensure that segregation takes place when non-family members are entering the home. The host should prepare some food and drink for the guest. Whether it's snacks or a meal, Food and drink can create unity and build love among people. If the guest is eating, the host should not finish eating before the guest. The guest may be hungry, and if they see the host finish eating before the guest, the guest may feel embarrassed, as they could be deemed to be greedy. While the guest is on the property, the host must ensure their needs are taken care of. For example, they may want to use the restroom or may want a space to pray. The guest should also not be demanding and should take into consideration the situation of the host. The guest and host should always maintain good manners and etiquette.

When listening to someone, you should focus your attention on them. You should try not to fidget, look elsewhere, or be occupied by other things. This can look rude to the person who is engaging in conversation with you. If you're in a rush, you should mention this politely to make the other party aware. When going to a guest's house, the host should mention if any food will be prepared or not to give a heads-up to the guest. They may have food prepared elsewhere, which may go to waste. Therefore, when going to a guest's house, consultation should be done prior to the meeting taking place, so both parties know what to expect.

Unfortunately, we see much selfishness in the Masjids. How ironic is this? As Muslims, we should be the best examples to our communities for our manners and etiquette. However, in my experience, I have seen the worst-behaved people in the mosque. Before going to the mosque, one should know its rules and values to obtain the highest level of reward. You must be clean. You cannot be smelling foul odours; this will displease Allah and will bother other worshippers. One should go to the mosque wearing the correct attire. Loose clothing, body entirely covered, and ready to pray. You should not wear clothing with pictures or logos of animals or humans in the mosque. There are many moments where I've seen people praying with clothing from particular brands that have animals as their logo. Prayer in this condition is disliked by Allah. You should enter the mosque with the right foot and recite the following Dua.

Transliteration:
Allaa-hum-maf-tah-lee-ab-waa-ba-rah-matik

Translation:
"O Allah! Open your doors of mercy for me."

While in the mosque, we should try to remain silent and totally avoid worldly conversations, as this is a sin. We should keep our interactions to a minimum, especially during prayer times. Of course, if there's an event at the mosque, such as a wedding, religious speeches, exhibitions, etc., then you will obviously have to interact with other people. This is different. During the times of the daily prayers, we see Muslims in Majids, sitting with their legs out and their feet pointing towards the Kabah. Some Muslims even leave the Quran on the floor or use it as a stand when getting up from the ground. This is an error and must be avoided. Do not pray in inconvenient spaces in the mosque. For example, right near the fire exit, entrances, or at the back, people cannot pass you. If you see a fellow Muslim in prayer, it is haram to walk in front of them or past them. "If the one crossing in front of a praying person knew what sin was upon him, it would be better for him to wait forty than walk across." Abu Al-Nadhr (one of the narrators of the hadith) said: I don't know whether he said forth days, months, or years. (Bukhari) Masjids should have some stands so worshippers may put them in front while praying so others can avoid the since. If you have something like a chair or pillar in front of you while praying, then it is permissible for others to walk past you.

Always try to display manners in a way that will benefit you spiritually as well as positively representing yourself to those around you, regardless of faith and colour. This includes keeping your word and promises. Do not keep promises that you cannot keep or may doubt. Breaking promises is a grave error in Islam. Do not give your word if you are in doubt. For example, if you tell someone you'll meet them at a certain time and date, make sure you stick to that agreement. If you cannot attend, Notify them in advance to avoid further inconvenience. If you cannot keep your word or promise, this gives a negative representation of you and your personal traits. Therefore, as a Muslim, you must be careful. People will think of you as a two-faced, liar, and untrustworthy individual if you cannot keep your word. Before you keep a promise or give someone your word, think about it first. There's no need to rush. Think about whether you can actually keep your word before you make any agreement. This leads me on to the next factor. If you take something from someone, make sure to give it back before the proposed date. This includes loans. Do not borrow money that you cannot repay. This will cause you distress and harm the party you borrowed from.

Be mindful when loaning to others; if you know they'll miss payments or they have a history of not paying money back to others, then most likely this same individual will still have the same behaviour with you. It is part of the Sunnah to look after yourself and your family first before helping others. Do not make any arrangements that will leave you in difficulty. It's important to have a written contract or agreement for any lending you have done with others. It is best to have this document signed by both the lender and receiver, along with witnesses from both parties. In the event case a death occurs and you need to be repaid by the family, the document will clearly state the details of the transaction. This will further mitigate conflicts among families if they arise. The person giving the loan should be understanding of any difficulties the borrower may face. An emergency may occur when he needs to use the funds elsewhere, which may mean missed payments. You should always expect the worst-case scenario when loaning someone money, regardless of who they are and how long you've known them. If you know you won't be able to tolerate a single missed payment, it is best not to loan that money. The person or group asking for the loan should also be understanding of others situations and should not get angry or think negatively if those they're asking cannot give them the loan.

Manners towards one's teacher are also an important aspect of Islam. If anything, this is one of the most important aspects of any Muslim journey. The problem with many Muslims in the modern era is that, at a young age, we either send our children to the evening classes at the local mosque or we have a private tutor to teach them. However, when they reach the teenage years, parents are the ones who come up with excuses for their children to miss the Masjid classes. I've been teaching children, teenagers, and adults Islamic studies since I was 17. I've seen many excuses. Either the family has gone shopping, or they're having some sort of family party at a relative's house, and so on. Maybe, once here and there on the odd occasion, you may need to attend a family gathering or outing of such nature, which is totally fine. However, on a regular basis, this is a recipe for disaster.

Being a teacher at masjids myself, I know the feeling when you genuinely try to nurture students and look out for the best in their well-being, but negative influences from parents, family, and friends affect the child's attendance and progress at the masjid or home learning. Therefore, when following the religion, one must ensure he or she is respecting the teacher at all times. You cannot learn Islam without a teacher. Regardless of how many books you read, how many YouTube videos you watch, and how much you Google it, Real knowledge of Islam comes from a good teacher.

We live in times where knowledge is easily accessible, but our communities lack wise individuals. It's easy to translate verses of the Quran or the Hadith (traditions of the Prophet, peace be upon him). But it's not easy to explain them without wisdom. This is why following the Awliyah (friends of Allah) is important. We will delve into the topic of following a spiritual guide later on in the book. But for now, coming back to my main point of respecting the teacher, The teacher should be honoured at all times. As humans, it is natural for people to have faults. There are some defects that an Islamic teacher should not have. For example, using students for their own self-interest. Being greedy for worldly gains, backbiting, slandering, telling tales, and more. If you have teachers with these faults, then one must search for a new teacher. You will not benefit from these individuals, as internally, these people have conflicts. On one hand, they have religious knowledge, which is supposed to humble a person and spiritually uplift them, yet on the other hand, they suffer from basic etiquette. As a new Muslim or someone interested in Islam, God has put a light inside you to seek knowledge about Islam. This is also a form of guidance. Therefore, when selecting a teacher, make sure they have the right etiquette and educational background.

Chapter 4

Tahara (Purification)

The Prophet, peace be upon him, said, "Cleanliness is half faith." This should be enough for you to know how important it is to be clean in Islam and to remain in that state as much as possible. Without cleanliness, many acts of worship are not accepted. Such as prayer, tawaf (circulation of the Kabah), and walking or running between Mount Safa and Marwa during Umrah or Hajj. Scholars further say that there are fewer blessings in acts such as reciting Tasbeeh (reciting on prayer beads) without Wudu (ablution), although one does not need Wudu (ablution) for this. However, the more consciousness one takes in their worship, the more reward they will receive, In-Sha-Allah (God willing), as you will be rewarded according to your intentions as stated by the prophet, peace be upon him:

إِنَّمَا الْأَعْمَالُ بِالنِّيَّاتِ، وَإِنَّمَا لِكُلِّ امْرِئٍ مَا نَوَى، فَمَنْ كَانَتْ هِجْرَتُهُ إِلَى دُنْيَا يُصِيبُهَا أَوْ إِلَى امْرَأَةٍ يَنْكِحُهَا، فَهِجْرَتُهُ إِلَى مَا هَاجَرَ إِلَيْهِ

Translation: *"The reward of deeds depends upon the intentions and every person will get the reward according to what he has intended. So whoever emigrated for worldly benefits or for a woman to marry, his emigration was for what he emigrated for."* (Sahih al-Bukhari)

In order to know how to clean oneself, one must first know the types of uncleanliness and how to clean certain types of impurities known in Arabic as "Najasah." According to the Hanafi school of thought, There are two types of impurities. Major impurities, known as "Najasah Ghaleezah" in Arabic terminology.

Major impurities (Najasah Ghaleezah) include:

- Urine or stool of humans.

- Stools of animals

- Flowing blood from animals and humans.

- Pus

- Vomit

- Saliva from animals

- Alcohol

Minor Impurities (Najasah Khafeefah) include:

- Urine of animals that are Halal to eat, such as cows, chickens, camels, sheep, goats, lambs, etc.

- Droppings of birds that are Haraam to eat, such as a crow or falcon.

When praying, the body, clothes, and place of prayer must be clean of all the above. If any of the above major or minor impurities are found on the body, clothes, or place of prayer, then certain rules and regulations must be followed to clean up the dirtiness. If there are any major impurities (Najasah Ghaleezah), if they are greater in size than a 10 pence British coin, then prayer will be invalid. This same rule also applies if the major impurity is the same size as a 10-pence coin. However, if the major impurity is less than this size coin, then prayer is valid. However, it is part of the sunnah of the prophet, peace be upon him, to remove any dirt from the body, clothes, or place of prayer.

Regarding the minor impurity (Najasah Khafeefah), If the impurity is less than a quarter of a section of a piece of clothing, such as the sleeve or leg, or smaller in size than a body part, such as the hands or feet, then prayer will be valid. However, if the minor impurity (Najasah Khafeefah) is more than a section of garment or greater than a body part, then the prayer will be invalid and the prayer must be repeated. When washing the clothes, if any of the impurities are still visible, then they must be washed again until the impurities are not visible.

Istinjaa

Istinjaa is the cleansing of the excretory passages. Istibraa is obligatory—stopping the falling of najaasah (impurities). Even then, Istinjaa is Sunnah, even if one is completely sure that no najaasah (impurities) will fall. It is permissible to perform istinjaa with a tissue, stone, or anything like it. It is enough to wipe until one is clean. No specific number is required for Istinjaa, even though some numbers are mentioned in the ahadeeth. It is better to use water even if no najaasah remains. The virtues of this are mentioned in the Qur'an with regard to the people of the Quba. If the impurity is beyond the exit, water must be used or any other purifying liquid.

NOTE: One must take care when becoming clean from impurities, especially in the case of urine and stool. Urine has been mentioned specifically as a reason for punishment in the grave. There are also ahadeeths mentioning taking care of urine.

Etiquettes of answering the call of nature

(1) Enter the restroom with the left foot and recite the Dua:

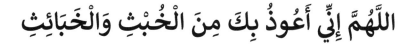

اللَّهُمَّ إِنِّي أَعُوذُ بِكَ مِنَ الْخُبْثِ وَالْخَبَائِثِ

Transliteration:
"Alla-humm-a-In-nee-a-udhu-bika-minal-khu-b-uthi-wal-kha-baa-ith"

Translation:
"Oh Allah, I take refuge with you from all evil and evil-doers."

One can recite the Dua in the bathroom so long as they are away from the impure area and so long as they are not performing the action of reliving themselves.

(2) Do not face the Qiblah when reliving oneself, and do not face your back towards it. If a toilet is built that way, then one should move slightly left or right or have this toilet rebuilt in an appropriate way.

(3) One should sit down and answer the call of nature. While standing and reliving oneself while standing is not Haraam, it is Makruh Tahrimi, i.e., it is sinful.

(4) One should not mention Allah's name, nor should one give or return Salaam.

(5) One should perform Istibraa (to make the urethra free of drops of urine) and Istinjaa (to clean the private parts of any urine or stool)

(6) Exit the bathroom with the right foot and recite the Dua: "Ghufraan Alhamdulillah Alladhee Adh-Haba Annil Adhaa 'Afaani"

Bathing (Ghusl)

The Necessitates of Ghusl: Things That Make Ghusl obligatory:

Things that obligate Ghusl are:

1. Emission of semen, accompanied by spurting and excitement, from a man or a woman.

2. Contact between the two private parts even without ejaculation. (Not if clothed.)

3. Haydh (Menstruation)

4. Nifas (post-natal bleeding)

When bathing or showering, it is recommended to recite the supplication for bathing or showering.

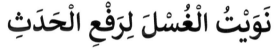

Transliteration:
Na-way-tul-ghu-sla-li-raf-il-hadath

Translation:
"I intend to perform Ghusl for the purpose of removing major impurity."

There are three mandatory acts when bathing or showering.

1. The mouth must be rinsed at least once.

2. The nose should be cleaned at least once.

3. Wash the entire body.

Using your right hand, you should put water in your mouth, gargle, and rinse your mouth three times. Using your right hand once again, you should put water in your nose, and using your left hand, pinkie finger, and thumb, you must insert them into the nostrils and clean as much as you can three times. Lastly, the entire body must be wet when bathing or showering. Not a single hair should be left dry. Even if one hair is left dry, then ghusl (bathing or showering) is incomplete. If bathed or showered according to the sunnah, this will suffice for Wudu (ablution), and prayer can be completed as long as the above actions, including reciting the supplication, are completed.

Cleaning of the nostrils and private parts should be done with the left hand, as the right hand is used for consuming food and drink. It is recommended to perform Wudu (ablution) while bathing. It is Sunnah to wash the entire body, starting with pouring water over the head three times. Then wash the right shoulder three times, followed by the left. You can wash the entire body in any order you may, as this is enough to fulfil the compulsory act of bathing. However, if done in the order of the Sunnah, you will be rewarded more, In-Sha-Allah. It is also recommended to rub around the body after water is poured, so you are certain that the entire body is completely wet and any impurities have been removed.

There are a few disliked (Makrooh) acts when bathing. One should not waste water or use more than is needed. You shouldn't converse with others while bathing or performing Wudu (abduction). Cleaning body parts with the right hand is disliked, as is staring from the left side of the body, as this is against the Sunnah.

Wudu (Ablution)

يَـٰٓأَيُّهَا ٱلَّذِينَ ءَامَنُوٓاْ إِذَا قُمْتُمْ إِلَى ٱلصَّلَوٰةِ فَٱغْسِلُواْ وُجُوهَكُمْ وَأَيْدِيَكُمْ إِلَى ٱلْمَرَافِقِ وَٱمْسَحُواْ بِرُءُوسِكُمْ وَأَرْجُلَكُمْ إِلَى ٱلْكَعْبَيْنِ ج

Translation:

" O believers! When you rise up for prayer, wash your faces and your hands up to the elbows, wipe your heads, and wash your feet to the ankles" – Surah Maidah (Chapter 5 of the Quran)

The Prophet peace be upon him said, prayer is the key to Paradise and the key to prayer (Salaah) is Wudu (Ablution) (al-Tirmidhi, Hadith 4).

This hadith is more than enough for us to understand the importance of Wudu and how one must make their ablution according to the Sunnah. Many times, people have come to me saying they cannot concentrate during their prayer. I told them to focus as much as you can during Wudu (ablution), and I can almost guarantee you that you'll be able to be more attentive and conscious during your prayer. Alhamdulilah (All praise be to Allah), this tends to often work. People think Wudu is just washing parts of the body three times, and that's it. There is a secret wisdom in Wudu: one must be attentive before and while performing Wudu. The solution is to prepare to communicate with your creator. Therefore, utmost care must be taken.

Praying, touching a copy of the Quran, and performing the circulation (Tawaaf) around the Kabah can only be completed when one has Wudu (ablution). Without Wudu, the above forms of worship will be void.

Steps of Wudu

1. Start by saying 'Bismillah' (in the name of Allah).

2. Wash the right hand up the wrists three times. Making sure you clean in between the fingers and cleaning the nails.

3. Gargle and rinse your mouth three times.

4. Clean the nose three times. Using the right hand, water should be entered into the nostrils. The left pinkie and left thumb should be used to clean the insides of the nose.

5. Wash the entire face three times, from the hairline to under the chin and earlobe to earlobe.

6. Wash your right arm three times. Starting from the tips of the fingers up to and including the elbow.

7. Wash the left arm three times, following the method in step 6.

8. Wiping the hair. Wash and rinse the hands. Using the pinkie, ring, and middle fingers of both hands, wipe across the hair, starting from the bottom of the hairline and finishing at the back of the neck. Using the palms, as they'll still be wet, go over the sides of the hair. Using the thumb, wipe over the edge of the ears, then use the index finger to clean the inside of the ears. Finish this step by using the back of the hands to wipe the neck.

9. Wash your right foot three times. Make sure the area in between the toes is cleaned, as well as the heel and bottom of the feet. You should wash just above the ankle.

10. Wash your left foot three times, following the steps above.

Once finishing Wudu, you should recite the following dua as well as durood shareef (peace and blessings on the Prophet, peace be upon you).

أَشْهَدُ أَنْ لَاَّ إِلَهَ إِلَّا اللهُ وَحْدَهَ لَا شَرِيكَ لَهَ وَأَشْهَدُ أَنَّ مُحَمَّداً عَبْدُهُ وَرَسُولُهُ

Transliteration:
'Ash-hadu-al-laa-ilaa-ha-ill-alla-ahu-wah-dahu-laa-sha-ree-ka-lahu-wa-ash-hadu-anna-mu—hammadan-ab-duhu-wa-ra-soo-luhu.

Translation:
"I bear witness that none has the right to be worshipped but Allah alone, Who has no partner; and I bear witness that Muhammad is His slave and His Messenger"

اَللّٰهُمَّ اجْعَلْنِي مِنَ التَّوَّابِيْنَ وَاجْعَلْنِي مِنَ الْمُتَطَهِّرِيْنَ

Transliteration:

Allaa-hum-maj-alnee-mi-nat-taw-waa-bee-na-waj-alnee-mi-nal-mu-ta-tah-hireen.

Translation:

"O Allah, make me among those who turn to You in repentance, and make me among those who are purified"

Mandatory Acts of Wudu

There are 4 mandatory acts in Wudu. If any one of them is missed, then ablution (Wudu) will be incomplete and Salaah (Prayer) will be invalid.

1. Washing the entire face.

2. Washing both arms.

3. Wiping of the hair.

4. Washing both feet.

Sunnah Acts of Wudu

As well as mandatory acts, there are also Sunnah acts, which are in Wudu. These must obviously be done and cannot be left out, in my opinion. Muslims must always make their best efforts to maximise their rewards and follow the path of the prophet, peace be upon him.

1. Making an intention to perform an ablution.

2. Reciting Bismillah.

3. Washing of the hands up to the wrist three times.

4. Use a miswaak/siwaak (toothstick) to clean the teeth.

5. Washing of the mouth and gargling. Remember, water should be put in the mouth using the right hand.

6. When cleaning the nose, it is advised to slightly sniff in some of the water; this ensures that water travels up the nose, allowing it to be properly cleaned. Remember to use the left hand for cleaning the nose and the right hand to insert water into the nose.

7. If a male has a beard or any facial hair, then it is important to remember to run the fingers through the beard to ensure it is wet.

8. Cleaning in between the toes and fingers. In Arabic, this is known as "Khilaal.".

9. Washing each body part three times. Washing the body part once is mandatory.

10. Wiping the entire head with wet hands. Wiping a quarter is mandatory.

11. Wiping both ears with wet hands.

12. Always start with the right and finish with the left of the body parts.

13. The order mentioned above for Wudu is according to the Sunnah. Technically, performing Wudu in any order will be valid, but doing it in the order set above is the Sunnah way, which is more rewarding.

14. To recite the dua (supplication) after finishing Wudu. This is mentioned above.

Disliked Acts of Wudu

In Wudu, there are a few acts that are disliked by Allah (Makrooh). It is important to know these, as they may increase rewards and may spiritually help you. For example. To talk unnecessarily during Wudu is disliked. When preparing for worship, your preparation should be done with as much concentration and consciousness as possible. As mentioned earlier, to make oneself spiritually uplifted, the more effort that is put into worship, the more you may be blessed and rewarded, In-Sha-Allah. Wasting water is disliked when making Wudu. We should think about all the people around the world for whom water is scarce. We should feel privileged that even with our heavy sins, Allah has given us many blessings in life.

Translation:

"Surely the wasteful are like brothers to the devils. And the Devil is ever ungrateful to his Lord. (Surah al-Isra, Verse 27)"

While wiping our body parts during Wudu, we should leave the tap on; this is what causes a waste of water. On the other hand, using so little water that barley does not flow over the skin is also disliked. Washing the left side first before the right is disliked, as this is against the Sunnah. Furthermore, while cleaning the nose, using the right for the cleaning is Makrooh. Splashing water on the face should be avoided. While washing the face, both hands should be used, and water should be used gently.

Nullification of Wudu

The Invalidators of Wudu: The incidents that invalidate Wudu' are:

- Anything that exits from the two paths.

- This includes anything that exits any of the passages, whether natural or unnatural (excluding the passing of wind from the front passage).

- A universal rule is: "Wudu is necessary for that which exits and not that which enters." (Exception: taking anything that takes the senses away.).

- When urinating, one should take care and do Istibraa (making the uterus free of drops of urine) so drops of urine do not drip.

- For those who have gas problems: if they are not sure whether they have passed wind or not, Wudu is only necessary if one hears a sound or there is a smell.

- For people who do not have problems, any indication of passing wind, even if there is no sound or smell, will break the WUDHU.

(2) blood, pus, or serum when they exit from the body and encroach on a place where it is incumbent to purify.

- Flowing blood or pus (from a wound) or flowing serum (an amber-coloured, protein-rich liquid that separates out when blood clots) breaks the Wudu.

- If one sees blood on the body but it doesn't exit the wound (i.e., it is not flowing), then the Wudu is intact.

(3) Vomit, if it was a mouthful.

- Vomit that does not amount to a mouthful will not break the Wudu.

- If someone vomits in small amounts at regular intervals and the amount reaches a mouthful, Wudu will be invalidated.

1. Sleeping lying down, leaning [on one's side], or reclining such that if it were removed, he would fall.

2. Loss of consciousness through fainting or insanity.

3. Laughter in any prayer containing Ruku and Sujud (i.e., excluding the funeral prayer).

Things that do not break Wudhu:

There are many things that do not break the Wudhu. A few will be mentioned below:

- Bleeding that does not exit the wound (e.g., dry blood in the nose)

- Vomiting (not to the extent of a mouthful):

- Sleeping while performing Ruku or Sujud.

- Feeling really sleepy (e.g., slumber).

- Breast-feeding

How to perform Wudu (ablution)

1. One should start with the name of Allah. For the Prophet, peace be upon him, said:

"there is no prayer for the one who does not have wudu, and there is no wudu for the one who does not mention allah's name upon it. This hadith is quoted in numerous famous compilations. Such as Ibn Majah and Abu Dawood. Therefore, before starting Wudu (ablution), one should recite:

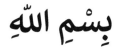

Transliteration:
Bis-mil-laah

Translation:
In the name of Allah

It is recommended to keep reciting this as you're doing your Wudu (ablution). This helps keep focus on your assignment. One should avoid any form of talking when doing their Wudu (ablution).

2. Wash hands Starting with the right hand, ensure the nails in between the fingers and wrist are thoroughly washed. This should be done three times. The right hand first three times, then the left hand three times.

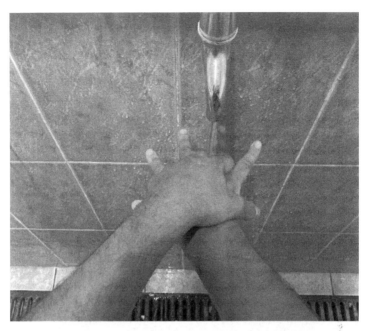

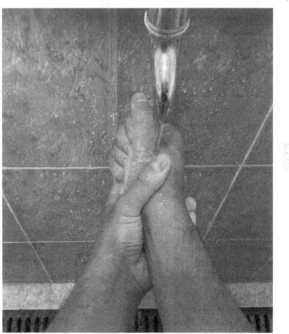

3. Rinse mouth and gargle.

Using your right hand, place water in your mouth and rinse your mouth. Place water again in your mouth to gargle. This should be done three times.

4. Clean nose

Place water using your right hand into the nose. Using the thumb and pinkie finger of the left hand, you should Insert them into the nostrils to clean.

5.Wash face

Wash the entire face three times.

NOTE: Those who have a beard should run their fingers through their beard to ensure it is wet. When washing the face, one should ensure the entire face from bottom of the hairline, to under the chin is wet.

6.Wash arms

Wash the right arm three times and then left arm three times. You should wash just above the elbows. To ensure the entire arm is wet.

7. Wash hair, ears and back of neck

Wash both hands. Using the pinkie, ring, and middle fingers of both hands, you should start from the top of the head (where your hairline begins) and wipe all the way until the back of the head (or where your hair stops, if you have long hair). Your palms will still be wet. Starting from the back of the head, you should wipe the sides of the hair and finish at the front. You will then use your index fingers to clean the insides of your ear. Then use the thumbs to clean the back of the ear. You will then finish this part of Wudu (ablution) by using the back of your hands to wipe over your neck. This is the only part where washing is permitted. Unlike other parts that have to be washed three times.

8. Wash feet

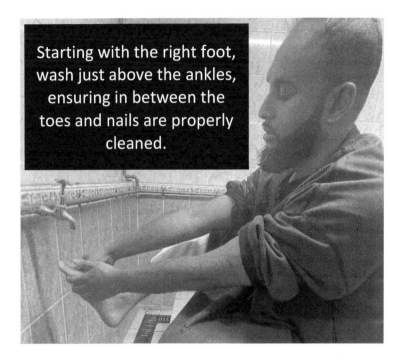

Starting with the right foot, wash just above the ankles, ensuring in between the toes and nails are properly cleaned.

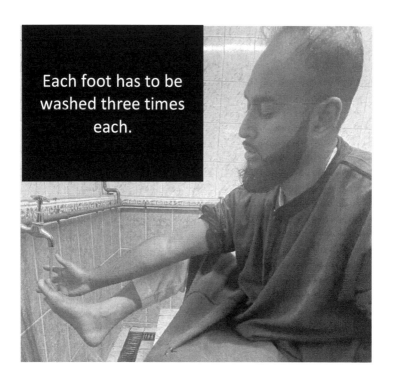

Each foot has to be washed three times each.

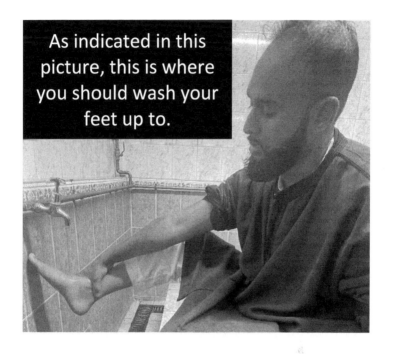

As indicated in this picture, this is where you should wash your feet up to.

Tayyammum (dry Ablution)

Dry ablution is another form of purification. However, this can only be performed in certain circumstances, as listed below. Things that nullify Wudu will also nullify Tayyamum. When water is found, your Tayyamum will automatically expire. Similarly, if Tayyamum is performed due to sickness, once the person has recovered, Tayyamum will be broken.

1. No water is to be found within a mile radius.

2. When one is unwell, using water will make the sickness worse.

3. If one is late for a Janazah (funeral prayer) or the last Jamaat for Eid prayers, there's a higher chance of missing the congregation due to performing Wudu.

Dry ablution can be performed using earthly materials such as soil, sand, brick, sand, and dust.

How to perform Tayyamum (dry Ablution)

1. Make it your intention to perform Tayyamum.

2. To strike both hands together on any of the materials.

3. Wipe both hands over the entire face.

4. Strike both hands once again at the material used.

5. Wipe over both arms, starting from the tips of the fingers and finishing slightly above the elbow. The right arm should be done first.

Mandatory acts of Tayyamum

There are 3 Faraid's (mandatory) acts in Tayyamum.

1. Making the intention to perform Tayyamum.

2. To strike both hands and wipe the face.

3. To strike both hands again and to wipe over the arm.

Prophetic (Sunnah) acts whilst performing Tayyamum

1. To recite Tasmiya.

2. Following the sequence mentioned above, this is Sunnah.

3. Not to delay actions in between.

4. To strike the surface firmly with the hands, then to shake off any earth.

5. Spreading the fingers when hitting the ground.

6. Moving the hands forward and backward when hitting the surface

NOTE: If you have to perform dry ablution, It wlll be nullified as soon as you have access to water. Until they, whatever, nullify Wudu will nullify dry ablution.

Other Important Notes on Purification

The Prophet, peace be upon him, mentions in a hadith that there are 10 acts that are natural acts of cleanliness for humans:

Aisha reported: The Messenger of Allah, peace and blessings be upon him, said, "Ten acts are part of natural instinct: trimming the moustache, letting the beard grow, using the toothstick, sniffing water into the nose, clipping the nails, washing the knuckles, removing hair from the underarms, shaving the pubic hair, and cleaning the private parts with water." Mus'ab said, "I forgot the tenth, except that it might be rinsing the mouth." Source: Ṣaḥīḥ Muslim 261

Thus, we draw the following conclusions based on this:

- Men should allow their beards to grow naturally, and it is disliked to shave them off. However, it should still be kept neat.

- Regarding the moustache, the recommendation is to trim and not let the moustache overflow.

- Mouth and dental hygiene are emphasised, with the use of a miswak (tooth stick) being an emphasised sunnah of the Prophet, peace be upon him.

- There are certain areas that should be taken extra care of so that no impurities remain. The hadith details these as the knuckles, the inside of the mouth, and the private parts.

- Cutting the nails, removing hair from the underarms, and removing pubic hair must be done within a minimum of 40 days. It is recommended to reduce the time between removals.

Hair Removal of Other Parts of the Body

- It is prohibited to pluck the hair of the eyebrows.

- Women are prohibited from shortening their hair so that it imitates that of a man.

- Both men and women must shave their any pubic/underarm hair on a regular basis.

Haydh (Menstruation)

1. **Minimum and Maximum Duration:** The minimum duration of haydh (menses) is three days, and the maximum is ten days.

2. **Acts During Haydh:** During menstruation, a woman is exempt from acts of worship such as prayer and fasting. She is required to make up missed fasts but not missed prayers.

3. **Ghusl (Ritual Bath):** Ghusl is obligatory at the end of the menstrual period to become ritually pure.

Nifaas (postpartum bleeding)

Definition: Nifas refers to the bleeding that occurs after childbirth.

Duration: The maximum duration of nifas is forty days. If bleeding exceeds this period, it is considered istihadah (irregular bleeding).

Acts During Nifas: Similar to haydh, a woman in a state of nifas is exempt from acts of worship, and she is required to make up missed fasts but not missed prayers.

Ghusl: Ghusl is obligatory at the end of postpartum bleeding to regain ritual purity.

Istihadah (irregular bleeding)

Definition: Istihadah refers to irregular, non-menstrual bleeding.

Duration: There is no fixed duration for istihadah. It continues until the bleeding ceases.

Acts During Istihadah: A woman experiencing istihadah is required to perform regular acts of worship, such as prayer and fasting, but she must perform wudu (ablution) for each prayer.

Ghusl: Ghusl is not obligatory at the end of istihadah. It is recommended, but not required.

Chapter 5

Salaah (Prayer)

Five daily prayers

The 2nd pillar in Islam, is Salaah (Prayer). There are 5 daily prayers which all Muslims must pray every day.

1. Fajr (Dawn Prayer)

Fajr prayer starts when light first appears in the sky. This is also known as "true dawn." The Arabic term for true dawn is "Subhe-Saadiq." The timing of this prayer ends when the sun begins to rise. Fajr prayer consists of 4 Rakats split into two sections. 2 Rakat Sunnah, and 2 Rakat (units): Fard (mandatory).

2. Zuhur (Afternoon Prayer)

Zuhur prayer begins when the sun is at its peak point in the sky. According to the Hanafi school of thought, prayer for Zuhur ends when the shadow of an object is double its size. Zuhur prayers consist of 12 units. Broken down into four sections. 4 Rakat Sunnah, 4 Rakat Fard, 2 Rakat Sunnah, and 2 Rakat Nafl (optional).

3. Asr (Mid-Afternoon Prayer)

The time for Asr prayer starts when Zuhur ends. Asr prayer is made up of 8 rakats divided into two sections. 4 Rakat Sunnah and 4 Rakat Fard. In the Hanafi school of law, after the mandatory 4 Rakat of Asr, it is disliked to offer optional (Nafl) prayers or any other prayers at this time until Maghrib has been prayed.

4. Maghrib (Sunset Prayer)

The time for Maghrib starts when dusk appears. Maghrib prayer time ends when the sky is in total darkness. Maghrib prayers consist of 7 Rakat split into 3 divisions. 3 Rakat Fard (mandatory), 2 Rakat Sunnah, and 2 Rakat Nafl (optional).

5. Isha (Night Prayer)

The time of Isha begins when Maghrib finishes and ends until Fajr of the next day starts. Isha is the longest prayer, which has 17 Rakat, divided into 4 sections. 4 Rakat, Sunnah, 4 Rakat Fard, 2 Rakat Nafl, 2 Rakat Sunnah, 3 Rakat Witr (Obligatory), and 2 Rakat Nafl.

NOTE:

It is important to note that there are three certain times when prayer is impermissible:

1. Praying during sunrise is disliked. In all local mosque timetable prayers, you will find prayer times as well as the time for sunrise. No prayer should be prayed until the sun has risen. Which is approximately 30 minutes. The timings for sunrise can also be found on weather and prayer apps on a smartphone, tablet, etc. You should try to use the most accurate one. However, to be on the safe side, it is best to use the local mosque (Masjid) prayer calendar.

2. During the highest peak of the sun (midday), also known as "Zawaal,".

3. According to Hanafi law, unless you are praying the Asr of that day, no prayer should be performed approximately 25 minutes before the start of Maghrib (sunset).

Types of Sunnah

With the five daily prayers, there are two different types of Sunnah prayers. One is called "Sunnah Muakkadah." This translates into English as "emphasised Sunnah." Leaving out a Sunnah muakkadah is a sin. The Sunnah prayers below, which are classified as Sunnah Muakkadah, are all the Sunnah prayers, except the 4 Rakat sunnah (units) of Asr and the 4 Rakat sunnah (units) of Isha. The rest of the sunnah prayers across all five daily prayers must be prayed at all times. Unless, you fit the criteria of a traveller (Musaafir). To be classified as a traveller, one must travel at least 48 miles. Once you are a traveller, you will pray all mandatory units which are 4 rakat in half. For example, Zuhur, Asr and Isha has 4 rakat which are mandatory. You must then pray 2 rakats instead of 4. As a traveller you are still obliged to perform the 3 rakat Witr prayer.

Mandatory conditions of Salaah (Prayer)

Now we know the times, names of the daily prayers, and how many units each prayer consists of. We are now going to take a look at the obligatory acts that must be carried out before and during the prayer.

Before Praying:

1. Purification of the body.

The body must be clean in order for Salaah (prayer) to be valid. Ablution must be carried out before prayers unless one has completed ghusl (bathing or showering) according to the Sunnah (including the recitation of the invocation that must be read during a shower or bath).

2.   Clean clothes.

The clothes must be clean. There should be no impurities of any kind on the clothes. It is important to note that when reliving oneself, one must take extra precautions to clean themselves to avoid impurities being left on the clothes. Such as drops of urine.

3.   Clean praying place.

The place where one is or will pray must be clean. This is why it is best to pray on a prayer mat.

4.   Covering the body.

The body must be covered when praying. For men, it is mandatory to cover from the navel to the bottom of the knee. For women, the whole body must be covered except the hands and face. This does not mean men have the ability to pray with a vest or anything similar (less clothed). When standing in front of Allah, one should take extra care of the clothes being worn and make sure the individual is appropriately dressed.

5.   Facing the Kabah/Qiblah.

Prayer will only be valid when facing the direction of the Kabah. This is why it is useful to always carry a compass (which can be installed in any smartphone), as well as knowing the bearings and which direction to face in your location.

6.   Timings.

You should pray at the prescribed time. When praying, one must know if the time clashes with any of the forbidden prayer times, which we discussed earlier.

7.   Intention.

You must have an intention for what you're praying for. For example, if you're praying 4 Rakat (units) of Zuhur Sunnah, then this is the intention you must have. This is to affirm to your inner self which prayer you will be praying.

During Prayer:

As well as before prayer, during prayer there are mandatory acts that must be carried out, or the prayer will be invalid. The list is as follows:

1. The first takbeer.

The first takbeer in prayer is mandatory. The first takbeer has many alternative names. Such as "Takbeer-Ul-Ulaa," "Takabeer-Tahreema," and "Takbeer-Ul-Awwal." They all translate to the "first takbeer." This is when you raise your hands to start the prayer and say, "Allahu Akbar.".

2. Standing (Qiyaam).

Standing in prayer is mandatory for those capable of doing so. One is permitted to pray while sitting if there is a valid reason.

3. Qiraat (Recitation).

One must recite either one long verse (long enough to equate to three short verses) from the holy Quran or at least three short verses. This is obligatory in the first two Rakat (units) of Fard (mandatory) prayer and obligatory for all Rakat if the prayer is Sunnah, Witr, or Nafl.

4. Ruku (Bowing).

Bowing in every Rakat (unit) is mandatory.

5. Sajdah (Prostration).

When prostrating, the nose and forehead must touch the ground together.

6. Jalsa (last sitting).

The final sitting at the end of the unit is mandatory.

7. Salaam (ending the prayer).

Ending the prayer by giving Salaam to the right and left is mandatory. When you do this, you are conveying the message of peace to both angels on both sides of the shoulder.

Wajib Acts of Salaah

It is necessary to perform the Wajib acts in prayer. Missing out on any of these acts will require one to repeat the prayer again. However, if missed out accidentally, one can perform Sajida Sahu (prostration of forgetfulness) towards the end of the prayer.

Here is a list of the Wajib acts in prayer:

1. Recite Surah Al-Fatiha in the first two rakats (units) of a 3 and 4 unit salah and in all the rakats of witr and nafl prayers.

2. After reciting Al-Fatiha in the first two rakats of a 3 and 4 unit salah and in all rakats of witr and nafl (optional) prayers, recite another surah, which can either be three short verses or one long verse.

3. Recite Al-Fatiha first and then another surah.

4. Perform actions that occur more than once, one after the other; for example, go for the second sajdah right after the first sajdah.

5. Perform all acts of salah with moderation and tranquilly.

6. Pray the tashahhud in the first sitting (after raising one's head from the second sajdah of the second rakat) and also in the last sitting.

7. Stand for the third rakat immediately after finishing reciting tashahhud.

8. Include the Qunut Dua in the morning prayer.

9. Utter the Takbir during the Eid prayers.

10. For an imam to recite loudly in the prayers of Jum'ah, Eid, Tarawih, the witr of Ramadan, Fajr, and in the first two rakats of the Maghrib and Isha prayers A person praying alone has the

option to choose whether to recite these prayers loudly or silently.

11. For an Imam and an individual praying alone (munfarid) to recite silently in the last two rakat of Isha salah, the last rakat of Maghrib salah, and in Zuhr and Asr.

12. Conclude the prayer with two salaams.

Sunnah acts of Salaah

As these are optional acts of prayer, Missing any of them will still make the prayer valid. However, if one can complete the Sunnah acts (which everyone should be doing), it will certainly increase the reward of the prayer, as this is the way the Prophet, peace be upon him, prayed.

Below is a list of the Sunnah acts of prayer:

1. Stand straight without moving the head when saying the first Takbir.

2. Raise one's hands parallel to one's ears.

3. Face the palms and fingers of one's hands towards the Qiblah (Kabah).

4. When raising the hands for Takbir, leave the fingers as they are without spreading them apart or joining them together.

5. For a man, place the right hand over the left hand below one's navel by placing the palm of his right hand over the back of his left hand, clasping the wrists with the pinkie finger and thumb, and forming a ring.

6. Men should keep their feet four fingers apart.

7. Recite Thanaa.

8. Recite Tawuz (A'oothubillah) after Thanaa.

9. Recite Tasmiya (Bismillah) at the beginning of every Rakat before beginning Surah Al-Fatiha.

10. Say Ameen silently after Al-Fatiha.

11. Recite long surahs (Hujuraat to Burooj) in Fajr and Zuhr, medium-length surahs (Burooj to Bayyinah) in Asr and Isha Salah, and short surahs (Bayyinah to Naas) in Maghrib Salah.

12. Lengthen the first Rakat of the Fardh of Fajr only.

13. Say 'Subhaanarabbiyal 'adheem' three times in Ruku.

14. Grasp the knees with the hands in Ruku', spreading the fingers in Ruku for men.

15. Keep the legs straight in Ruku.

16. For men, keep their back flat in Ruku', making sure the head is level with their buttocks.

17. For men, the inner side of their arms should be away from their ribs.

18. Recite 'Sami-allaahu-liman-hamidah' when rising from Ruku'.

19. Pause for a while in the upright standing position after Ruku'.

20. Recite 'Rabba-na-walakal-hamd' in the upright standing position before Sajdah.

21. When making Sajdah, place the knees on the surface first, then hands, and then lastly the face, and then lift these parts in the reverse order when rising from Sajdah.

22. Say Takbir when going to and rising from Sajdah.

23. Place the head between the hands in sajdah.

24. Say 'Subhaana-rabbiyal-Alaa' three times in Sajdah.

25. For men, keep the stomach away from the thighs, the elbows away from the sides, and the forearms away from the ground.

26. Keep the two heels together in sajdah.

27. For men, spread the left foot and raise the right foot, making the toes face the Qiblah. The hands should be placed on the thighs.

28. Raise the index finger of the right hand when saying the words 'Ash-Hadu-Al-Lailaaha' of the Tashahhud and lower it when saying 'illallaahu'.

29. Recite Durood Ibrahim after the Tashahhud in the final sitting.

30. Follow it by reading a du'a, using words found in the Qur'an or Hadith. The du'a should not be in the words of common people.

31. Say Salaam to the right first, and thereafter to the left.

32. When saying Salaam, the imam should make the intention for all the people following him. For the one praying behind him, make an intention for the imam, together with the people, and for the one praying alone, make an intention for the angels only.

33. The salaam of the imam and those praying behind him should be simultaneous.

34. The latecomer in Salah should wait for the imam to finish his Salam first, then stand up to finish the remaining Salah.

Disliked (Makrooh) acts in Salaah

Makrooh is that which is disliked by Allah. If any Makrooh acts accidentally occur in prayer, the prayer will still be valid, but the reward will be lost. Below are some examples of disliked acts in prayer.

1. Closing your eyes (unless for concentration).

2. To look around.

3. Cracking the fingers.

4. Fidgeting with one's clothes.

5. Performing prayer with pictures of humans or animals on it. This includes the logos of brands that may also use animals in their logos.

66

Acts that break Salaah

1. To eat or drink in prayer.

2. Talking to others in prayer.

3. Turning away from the direction of the Kabah.

4. To make any unnecessary noise.

5. Stepping in front of the Imam (when praying in congregation).

Prostration of error (Sajidah Sahu)

If one or more Wajibaat (obligatory acts) are missed in prayer (regardless of whether it's intentional or not), then one has to perform the prostration of error (Sajidah Sahu) towards the end of the prayer. If a wajib (obligatory act) is missed in prayer and the prostration of error is not performed, then that prayer will need to be performed again within its time. However, if the prostration of error is performed, then the prayer remains valid. This rule is only for Wajib acts, not Fard (mandatory) acts. If a mandatory act is missed in prayer, then the prayer will need to be prayed again.

Jummuah Prayer (Friday congregational prayers)

Friday prayers must be performed in congregation. In previous eras, the Jumuah prayers would usually be prayed at the grand mosque of each city (the main mosque). One of the purposes of this was to keep Muslims united and the residents of the city aware of any major announcements. However, over the centuries, this norm has changed due to the location and convenience of the masses. Unless there's a valid reason, one should not miss Jumuah. In the west, Muslims will face a tough decision to pray Jumuah due to working times and the clash of the prayers. However, relevant efforts must be made. The rest is in the hands of Allah. I have included a list of Sunnah's that the Prophet peace be upon him would do, especially for Jumuah.

1. Clip nails.

2. To wear nice, clean clothes. In accordance with Islamic guidelines. For example, no foul words, slogans, or pictures.

Loose garments to conceal the body shape. This is for both men and women.

3. Recite Durood Shareef as many times as possible.

4. Going to the mosque early.

5. Reciting Surah Al-Kahf.

How to pray Jummuah prayers

4 Rakat (units) Sunnah Muakkadah

2 Rakat (units) Fard prayers (mandatory)

4 Rakat (units) Sunnah Muakkadah

2 Rakat (units) Sunnah Muakkadah

2 Rakat (units) Nafl (optional)

Note: Sunnah should not be missed. Sunnah Muakkadah is a strongly advised Sunnah. In between the first 4 Rakat Sunnah Muakkadah and the 2 Rakat Fard prayer, the Imam will deliver 2 sermons (Khutbah's), which are Waajib (obligatory) to listen to. During the sermon, it is impermissible to talk and eat. No one should pray or do any form of activity other than listen during the khutbah (sermon). Even if you do not understand the sermon, you should still not talk. Furthermore, Jummah prayers is not obligatory for women.

How to perform the prayer

1. When stepping on to the prayer mat, one should read the dua (supplication) for the prayer mat. This is optional. The dua is:

إِنِّى وَجَّهْتُ وَجْهِىَ لِلَّذِى فَطَرَ ٱلسَّمٰوٰتِ وَٱلْأَرْضَ حَنِيْفًا وَمَآ أَنَا۠ مِنَ ٱلْمُشْرِكِيْنَ

Transliteration:
In-ni-waj-jahtu-waj-hiya-lil-lazhee-fa-ta-ras-sama-wati-wal-arda-hanee-faw-wa-ma-ana-mi-nal-mush-rikeen

Translation:
"Indeed I have made myself attentive towards him who has created the earth & sky & I surrendered to him. I am not one of those who associate something with Him."

2. Raise the hands and recite the Takbeer (Allahu Akbar) quietly.

3. Tie the hands and recite "Thanaa"

سُبْحَانَكَ اَللّٰهُمَّ وَبِحَمْدِكَ وَتَبَارَكَ
اسْمُكَ وَتَعَالٰى جَدُّكَ وَلَاۤ إِلٰهَ غَيْرُكَ

Transliteration:

Sub-ha-naka-alla-humma-wa-bi-ham-dika-wa-tabara-kas-
muka-wa-ta-ala-jad-duka-wa-la-ila-ha-ghai-ruk

Translation:

'Glory to you oh Allah, and with your praise, and blessed is
your name, and exalted is your majesty, and none has the
right to be worshipped but you"

NOTE: Women should place their hands on their chest with the right hand on top of their left hand

4.One should then recite "Tawuz" which is below:

أَعُوْذُ بِاللهِ مِنَ الشَّيْطَانِ الرَّجِيْمِ

Transliteration:
A-uzu-bi-llah-he-mi-nash-shay-taan-nir-ra-jeem

Translation:
"I seek refuge with Allah from the accursed Satan."

5.Then you should recite Tasmiya (Bismillah)

Transliteration:
Bis-mil-laa-hir Rahmaa-nir Raheem

Translation:
"In the name of Allah the most affectionate, the most merciful"

6.Then one should start reciting Surah Al-Fatiha (chapter 1 of the Quran) and any other Surah (chapter). With a minimum of three verses.

NOTE: If the prayer is 4 units and is a fard (mandatory) prayer, You will recite Surah Al-Fatiha and another Surah (chapter) or a minimum of three verses from the Quran in only the first two units. In the 3rd and 4th units, You will only recite Surah Al-Fatiha. If it is a four-unit prayer of Sunnah or Nafl, then you will recite Surah Al-Fatiha and another Surah, or a minimum of three verses in all four units. In a two-unit prayer, regardless if it is Sunnah or Fard, you will recite Surah Al-Fatiha and any other Surah (chapter) or any three verses from the Quran in both units. If it is a three-mandatory prayer, like the three units in Maghrib, Then, in the third unit, you are only required to recite Surah Al-Fatiha.

7.Once recitation of Surah Al-Fatiha and a minimum of three verses have been recited. You will then enter into Ruku (bowing). Whilst in Ruku you will recite three times. The below dua. One should try to keep the back and legs straight. Keeping the hands on ones knees.

سُبْحَانَ رَبِّيَ الْعَظِيَمِ

Transliteration:
Sub-haa-na-rab-bi-yal-azheem

Translation:
"Glory to my Lord the exalted"

8.After Ruku (bowing) you will then stand-up straight. Whilst in the motion from bowing to standing, you will read the below dua, once:

سَمِعَ اللهُ لِمَنْ حَمِدَه

Transliteration:
Sami-alla-hu-li-man-ha-mi-dah

Translation:
"Allah hears whoever praises him"

Once you have stood up straight (without tying your hands) you will read the dua (supplication)below once:

رَبَّنَا لَكَ الْحَمْدُ

Transliteration:
Rab-ba-naa-la-kal-hamd

Translation:

"Our Lord, all praise is due only to you"

Note: To avoid any confusion. When standing up straight from Ruku (bowing), there are two versions of the dua (supplication) circled above. The first one is above, and the second version is given below:

رَبَّناَ وَلَكَ الحَمْدُ

Transliteration:

Rab-ba-naa-wa-la-kal-hamd

Translation:

"Our Lord and all praise is due only to you."

9. From this position, you will go straight into Sujood (prostration), and read the below dua (supplication) three times.

Transliteration:
Sub-haa-na-rabi-al-ala

Translation:
"Glory is to my lord, the most high"

NOTE: Men should keep their elbows raised while in Sujood (prostration). The elbows should not be touching any other part of the body (including resting them on the thighs or legs). Women should keep their elbows rested on the floor while in Sujood (prostration).

10. You will then sit from Sajidah (Prostration) and read the following dua (supplication).

اَللّهُمَّ اغْفِرْ لِيْ وَارْحَمْنِيْ

Transliteration:
Alla-hum-magh-fir-lee-warr-ham-nee

Translation:
Oh Allah, forgive me and have mercy upon me.

NOTE: Each unit of prayer has 2 Sajidah's (prostrations). Once you have sat up from your first prostration. You will then go back into Sajidah (prostration) for the 2nd Sajidah.

NOTE: For men, they should sit on the left foot and the right foot should be standing. For women, they are allowed to sit on both feet, whilst sat in prayer.

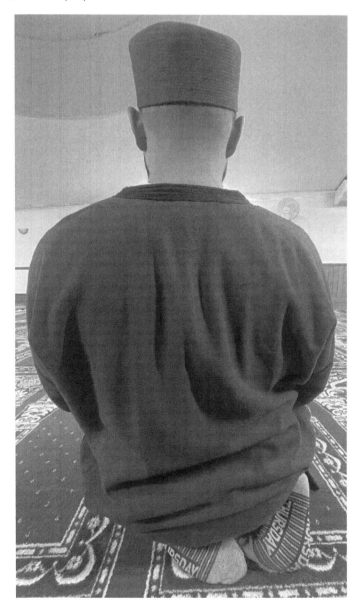

11. 2nd Sajidah (prostration). Just as the first Sajidah (prostration) you will do another Sajidah (prostration) and read the same dua (supplication) as stated in step 9.

NOTE: After this, Sajidah, you will then stand as shown in step 3. You do not need to raise your hands again (which is not permitted in the Hanafi school of thought). When you stand back up for the second unit, you stand with your hands folded and repeat the process.

12. Repeat steps 3,5,6,7,8,9,10,11

13. Jalsa (The sitting)

This will be your last sitting, if you are praying 2 Rakat (unit) prayer. If you are praying a 3 Rakat or 4 Rakat this will be your first sitting. When sitting, you will recite the following dua, known as "Tashahud" (testimony of faith).

اَلتَّحِيَّاتُ لِلَّهِ وَالصَّلَوَاتُ وَالطَّيِّبَاتُ اَلسَّلَامُ

عَلَيْكَ أَيُّهَا النَّبِيُّ وَرَحْمَةُ اللهِ وَبَرَكَاتُهُ

اَلسَّلَامُ عَلَيْنَا وَعَلٰى عِبَادِ اللهِ

الصَّالِحِيْنَ أَشْهَدُ أَنْ لَّا إِلٰهَ إِلاَّ اللهُ

وَأَشْهَدُ أَنَّ مُحَمَّدًا عَبْدُهُ وَرَسُولُهُ

Transliteration:
At-ta-hiy-ya-tu-lil-la-hi-was-sa-lawa-tu-wat-tay-yi-batu-As-sa-la-mu-

a-lay-ka-ay-yu-han-na-biy-yu wa-rah-ma-tul-lahi-wa- ba-ra-ka-tu-hu

As-sa-la-mu-a-lay-na-wa-alaa-ibaa-dil-la-hiss-sa-li-heena
Ash-ha-du-al-laa-i-la-ha-ill-alla-hu

Wa-ash-hadu-an-na-mu-ham-ma-dan-ab-duhu-wa-ra-su-lu-hu

Translation:

"All the best compliments and the prayers and the good things are for Allah. Peace and Allah's mercy and blessings be on you, O Prophet! Peace be on us and on the pious slaves of Allah, I testify that none has the right to be worshipped but Allah, and I also testify that Muhammad is Allah's slave and His Apostle."

NOTE: when reciting this dua (supplication) regardless of whether it is a 2 rakat, 3 rakat or 4 rakat prayer. You will raise your right index finger when reciting the phrase circled above.

Note: This is how the index finger should be raised. Once you have recited the word circled for the Tashahud (testimony of faith) supplication, you will put your right index finger back to how it originally was. If you are praying a 3 rakat or 4 rakat prayer, This is all you will read. Once you have finished reciting this dua (supplication), you will stand and continue with the prayer. If it is the final sitting of the prayer, then you will recite a further 2 dua's (supplications), which are as follows:

Durood-E-Ibrahim
(Salutations of Prophet Ibrahim peace be upon him)

اَللّٰهُمَّ صَلِّ عَلَى مُحَمَّدٍ وَّعَلٰى آلِ مُحَمَّدٍ
كَمَا صَلَّيْتَ عَلَى إِبْرَاهِيْمَ وَعَلٰى آلِ إِبْرَاهِيْمَ
إِنَّكَ حَمِيْدٌ مَّجِيْدٌ
اَللّٰهُمَّ بَارِكْ عَلَى مُحَمَّدٍ وَّعَلٰى آلِ مُحَمَّدٍ
كَمَا بَارَكْتَ عَلَى إِبْرَاهِيْمَ وَعَلٰى آلِ
إِبْرَاهِيْمَ إِنَّكَ حَمِيْدٌ مَّجِيْدٌ

Transliteration:
All-ahum-ma-salli-ala-mu-ham-madiw-wa-ala-ali-mu-ham-mad

Ka-maa-sal-lay-ta-ala-Ib-raa-hee-ma-wa-ala-ali-Ib-raa-heema-in-na-ka
ha-mee-dum-ma-jeed.

Alla-hum-ma-ba-arik-ala-mu-ham-madiw-wa-ala-ali-mu-ham-mad-ka-maa ba-rak-ta-

Ala-Ib-raa-hee-ma-wa-ala-ali-Ib-raa-heema-in-na-ka-ha-mee-dum-majeed

---

86

Translation:

"Oh Allah, bestow Your favour on Muhammad and on the family of Muhammad as you have bestowed Your favour on Ibrahim and on the family of Ibrahim. You are praiseworthy, most glorious.
O Allah, bless Muhammad and the family of Muhammad as you have blessed Ibrahim and the family of Ibrahim. You are praiseworthy, most glorious."

Dua-E-Masura

اَللّٰهُمَّ إِنِّي ظَلَمْتُ نَفْسِي ظُلْمًا كَثِيرًا
وَّلاَ يَغْفِرُ الذُّنُوْبَ
إِلَّا أَنْتَ فَاغْفِرْلِي مَغْفِرَةً
مِنْ عِنْدِكَ وَارْحَمْنِي
إِنَّكَ أَنْتَ الْغَفُوْرُ الرَّحِيْمُ

Transliteration:

Alla-hum-ma-in-nee-zha-lam-tu-naf-see-zhul-man-ka-thee-raau-wa-la-yagh-fi-ruzh-zhu-nu-ba

il-la-an-ta-fagh-fir-lee-magh-fi-ra-tam-min-indi-ka-war-ham-nee-in-na-ka-an-tal-gha-fu-rur-ra-heem

Translation:

"Oh Allah! I have greatly wronged myself and none forgives sins except ou, so grant me your forgiveness and have mercy on me. You are the forgiving, the merciful."

NOTE: You will only read these three dua's (supplications) in the last sitting of your prayer. For example, if you are praying for Rakat,. In the 2nd Rakat, you will only read the "Tashahud." On the 4th Rakat in the last sitting, you will read all three supplications, then end the prayer with Salaam (giving peace to the angels).

14. Salaam (giving peace to the angels)

To finish the prayer. You will first give Salaam (peace) to the angel on your right shoulder by turning your face to the right. Then you will turn your face to the left and give Salaam (peace) to the angel on the left shoulder. When doing this, you will recite the following:

Transliteration:
As-sa-laa-mu-a-lay-kum-wa-rah-ma-tul-laah

Translation:
May Allah's peace and mercy be upon you

NOTE: You will recite this whilst turning your head to the right, and recite again whilst turning your head to the left.

NOTE: After this Salaam (peace) on the left. Your prayer is officially finished.

One should make a Dua (supplication) after their prayer and ask Allah for forgiveness and anything (as long as it's Halal) else they desire.

3 Rakat (unit) Witr prayer

The 3 Rakat (unit) Witr prayer which is part of the Isha (night) prayer as a slightly different method. Usually in a 3 Rakat (unit) prayer like the mandatory 3 Rakat (unit) Maghrib prayer (sunset prayer). Requires you to read Surah Al-Fatiha (The opening chapter, chapter 1) and any other Surah (chapter) (or 3 consecutive verses of the Quran) in the first 2 Rakat (units) only and Surah Al-Fatiha, alone in the 3ʳᵈ Rakat (unit). However in the 3 Rakat (unit) Witr prayer. You are required to read Surah Al-Fatiha and another Surah (chapter) or 3 consecutive verses in every unit. On the 3ʳᵈ Rakat (unit) after you have recited another chapter (or 3 consecutive verses) instead of going to Ruku (bowing). You will raise your hands as shown in step 2, recite the Takbeer (Allahu-Akbar) fold your hands and recite what is known as:

Dua-E-Qunoot

اَللّٰهُمَّ إِنَّا نَسْتَعِيْنُكَ وَنَسْتَغْفِرُكَ وَنُؤْمِنُ بِكَ وَنَتَوَكَّلُ عَلَيْكَ وَنُثْنِي عَلَيْكَ الْخَيْرَ وَنَشْكُرُكَ وَلَا نَكْفُرُكَ وَنَخْلَعُ وَنَتْرُكُ مَنْ يَفْجُرُكَ

اَللّٰهُمَّ إِيَّاكَ نَعْبُدُ وَلَكَ نُصَلِّي وَنَسْجُدُ وَإِلَيْكَ نَسْعٰى وَنَحْفِدُ وَنَرْجُوْ رَحْمَتَكَ وَنَخْشٰى عَذَابَكَ إِنَّ عَذَابَكَ بِالْكُفَّارِ مُلْحِقٌ

Transliteration:

Alla-hum-ma-in-na-nas-ta-ee-nuka-wa-nas-tagh-fi-ruka-wa-nu'-mi-nu-bi-ka

Wa-na-ta-wak-kalu-a-lai-ka-wa-nuth-ni-a-lai-kal-khyr-wa-nash-ku-ru-ka

Wa-la-nak-fu-ru-ka-wa-nakh-la-u-wa-nat-ru-ku-mai-yaf-ju-ru-ka

Alla-hum-ma-iy-yaa-ka-na-bu-du-wa-laka-nu-salli-wa-nas-judu-wa-ilai-ka-

Nas-a-wa-nah-fizhu-wa-nar-ju-rah-ma-ta-ka-wa- nakh-shaa-azhaa-baka

In-na-azha-ba-ka-bil-kuf-faari-mul-hik

Translation:
Oh Allah! We implore You for help and beg forgiveness of you and believe in you and rely on you and extol you and we are thankful to you and are not ungrateful to you and we alienate and forsake those who disobey you.
Oh Allah! you alone do we worship and for You do we pray and prostrate and we betake to please you and present ourselves for the service in your cause and we hope for your mercy and fear your chastisement. Undoubtedly, your torment is going to overtake infidels.

NOTE: With the longer Dua's (supplications), I have tried to space them out more so they are easier to read and memorise. For those who are new Muslims, I understand the longer Dua's (supplications) could be tough to memorise. However, when recited regularly, these will become easier to read and know by memory. You can try to break it down into smaller portions to make it easier to read and memorise.

When it comes to reciting another Surah (chapter) or any three consecutive verses of the Quran throughout certain units of prayer, I should clarify that one is permitted to recite one verse of the Quran as one of the additional verses recited after Surah Al-Fatiha (depending on which prayer you are praying). However, that one verse must be equivalent to three short verses. For example, if one long verse from the Quran equates to three lines of the Quran, then that will suffice. The easiest way is to memorise the short Surah's (chapters of the Quran) given towards the end of this book.

Janazah (funeral) prayer

In the Hanafi school of thought, the Janazah (funeral) prayer should only be participated in by men. The funeral prayer is different from the daily prayers. In Janazah (funeral) prayer, there are 4 Takbeers; there is no Azaan (call to prayer); there's no Ruku (bowing); or Sujood/Sajidah (prostration). Janazah (funeral) prayer is always prayed in silence. So when reciting the Dua's (supplications), they should be recited silently, and the lips should be moving. As shown in steps 2 and 3 of the daily prayers, You will make the intention that you are praying a Janazah (funeral) prayer. You will then raise your hands and recite the Takbeer. The Imam will recite the Takbeer out loud for the congregation to follow. This will be the first Takbeer out of the four, and fold them. After each Takbeer is recited, you will not raise your hands. Your hand will always remain folded when performing Janazah (funeral) prayer.

You will first recite "Thanaa" like you would normally in prayer. However, the Thanaa for Janazah has a few more added extra words.

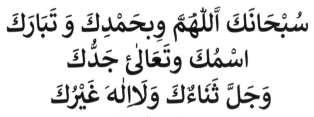

سُبْحَانَكَ اَللّٰهُمَّ وِبِحَمْدِكَ وَ تَبَارَكَ
اسْمُكَ وتَعَالٰئ جَدُّكَ
وَجَلَّ ثَنَاؤُكَ وَلَااِلٰهَ غَيْرُكَ

Transliteration:
Sub-Ha-Na-Ka-Alla-Hum-Ma-Wa-Bi-Ham-D-Ika-Wa-Ta-Ba-Ra-Kas-Muka-Wa-Ta-Alaa-Jad-Duka-
Wa-Jal-La-Sa-Na-Uka-Wa-La-Ila-Ha-Ghay-Ruk

Translation:

"Oh Allah! forgive those of us who are alive and those of us who are dead; those of us who are present and those of us who are absent; those of us who are young and those of us who are adults; our males and our females. Oh Allah! whomsoever you keep alive, let him live as a follower of Islam and whomsoever you cause to die, let him die as a believer"

Once this has been recited, the imam leading the prayer. Will recite out loud the 2nd takbeer (allahu-akbar). You will then recite durood-e-ibrahim as you do in the daily prayers.

Durood-E-Ibrahim (Salutations of Prophet Ibrahim) peace be upon him)

اَللّٰهُمَّ صَلِّ عَلٰى مُحَمَّدٍ وَّعَلٰى آلِ مُحَمَّدٍ
كَمَا صَلَّيْتَ عَلٰى إِبْرَاهِيْمَ وَعَلٰى آلِ إِبْرَاهِيْمَ
إِنَّكَ حَمِيْدٌ مَّجِيْدٌ
اَللّٰهُمَّ بَارِكْ عَلٰى مُحَمَّدٍ وَّعَلٰى آلِ مُحَمَّدٍ
كَمَا بَارَكْتَ عَلٰى إِبْرَاهِيْمَ وَعَلٰى آلِ
إِبْرَاهِيْمَ إِنَّكَ حَمِيْدٌ مَّجِيْدٌ

Transliteration:
All-ahum-ma-salli-ala-mu-ham-madiw-wa-ala-ali-mu-ham-mad
Ka-maa-sal-lay-ta-ala-Ib-raa-hee-ma-wa-ala-ali-Ib-raa-heema-in-na-ka
ha-mee-dum-ma-jeed.

Alla-hum-ma-ba-arik-ala-mu-ham-madiw-wa-ala-ali-mu-
ham-mad-ka-maa ba-rak-ta-
Ala-Ib-raa-hee-ma-wa-ala-ali-Ib-raa-heema-in-na-ka-ha-
mee-dum-majeed

Translation:

*"Oh Allah, bestow Your favour on Muhammad and on the
family of Muhammad as you have bestowed Your favour on
Ibrahim and on the family of Ibrahim. You are praiseworthy,
most glorious.*
*O Allah, bless Muhammad and the family of Muhammad as
you have blessed Ibrahim and the family of Ibrahim. You are
praiseworthy, most glorious."*

Once this has been recited the Imam will out loud recite the 3rd Takbeer.
You will then recite the following Dua (supplication):

اَللّٰهُمَّ اغْفِرْ لِحَيِّنَا وَمَيِّتِنَا وَشَاهِدِنَا
وَغَآئِبِنَا وَصَغِيْرِنَا وَكَبِيْرِنَا وَذَكَرِنَا وَأُنْثَانَا
اَللّٰهُمَّ مَنْ اَحْيَيْتَهُ مِنَّا فَأَحْيِهِ عَلَى الْإِسْلَامِ
وَمَنْ تَوَفَّيْتَهُ
مِنَّا فَتَوَفَّهُ عَلَى الْإِيْمَانِ بِرَحْمَتِكَ
يَا أَرْحَمَ الرَّحِمِيْنَ

Transliteration:
Allah-hum-magh-fir-lee-hay-yina-wa-mai-yi-tina-wa-shaa-hidina-wa-gha-
ibina-wa-saghee-rina-wa-inthaa-naa
Allah-humma-man-ah-yay-tahu-min-na-fa-ah-yihi-a-lal-islaam-wa-man
ta-waf-fai-tahu
Minna-fata-waf-fahu-a-lal-imaani-bi-rah-ma-tika-ya-ar-ha-mar-ra-hee-
mina

Translation:

"Oh, Allah. Forgive us, those that are alive, dead, present, absent young, adults, male and female. Oh Allah! Whom soever of us keep alive, let them lead their life on the path of Islam, and whoever you cause to die, let him die with Imaan with your mercy. Oh the best of those who are merciful."

Once this has been recited. The Imam will recite the 4th Takbeer loud (nothing is recited after the 4th Takbeer) after the 4th Takbeer the Imam will conclude the Janazah (funeral) prayer with the Salaam (peace) to the angels on the right and left. Whilst standing you will turn to the right and give Salaam (peace) to the angel on the right, and you will do the same on the left side. Just like how you turn your face in the daily prayers. You will recite the same Salaam (peace). Once this has been recited. This will conclude the Janazah (funeral) prayer.

اَلسَّلَامُ عَلَيْكُمْ وَرَحْمَةُ اللهِ

Transliteration:
As-sa-laa-mu-a-lay-kum-wa-rah-ma-tul-laah

Translation:
"May Allah's peace and mercy be upon you."

Eid prayer

Both Eid prayers have six Takbeers and two Rakat (units) that are mandatory. In the Hanafi school of thought, it is not necessary for women to pray the Eid prayer. However, there is no harm in women joining an Eid prayer congregation, as long as the facility is catered to women too.

Eid prayer always has to be prayed in congregation. In each unit of Eid prayer, there are three Takbeers. Once the intention for Eid prayer has been made, You will raise your hands, fold them, and recite "Thanaa" (not the one for Janazah/funeral).

سُبْحَانَكَ اَللّٰهُمَّ وَبِحَمْدِكَ
وَتَبَارَكَ اسْمُكَ وَتَعَالٰى جَدُّكَ
وَلاَ إِلٰهَ غَيْرُكَ

Transliteration:

Sub-ha-naka-alla-humma-wa-bi-ham-dika-wa-tabara-kas-

muka-

wa-ta-ala-jad-duka-wa-la-ila-ha-ghai-ruk

Translation:

"'Glory to you oh Allah, and with your praise, and blessed is your name, and exalted is your majesty, and none has the right to be worshipped but you"

Once this has been recited, The Imam will recite out loud two additional Takbeers (Allahu-Akbar). You will raise your hands and keep them by your side (not folding them) in each takbeer. When the Imam recites the 3rd Takbeer, you will fold your hands again. The Imam will recite from the Quran; you will then go into Ruku, then Sajidah (prostration), reading what you normally recite in the daily prayers. You will then stand for the second rakat. The Imam will recite from the Quran. instead of going straight to Ruku (bowing) after the recitation has finished. There will be 3 Takbeer's (Allahu-Akbar), which the Imam will recite out loud. In each of these 3 Takbeer's, you will raise your hands as shown in step 2 and keep them by your sides. On the 4th Takbeer, you will go into Ruku (bowing), and the rest of the prayer is as normal. Once the prayer is finished, On both Eid's, the Imam will deliver two sermons. These are mandatory to listen to, as they are part of the Eid prayer. Once the sermon has finished. The imam will conclude with a dua.

Chapter 6

Fasting (Sawm)

The third pillar of Islam, is Fasting in Ramadan. This chapter has been titled "Fasting" as we will cover not only the month of Ramadan, but also others Sunnah/Nafl (optional) fasts .

"The month of Ramadan in which was revealed the Quran, a guidance for mankind and clear proofs for the guidance and the criterion (between right and wrong). So whoever of you sights (the crescent on the first night of) the month (of Ramadan i.e. is present at his home), he must observe Sawm (fasts) that month…" [al-Baqarah 2:185]

The Messenger of Allah (peace and blessings of Allah be upon him) said: "There has come to you Ramadan, a blessed month which Allah has enjoined you to fast, during which the gates of heaven are opened and the gates of Hell are closed, and the rebellious devils are chained up. In it there is a night which is better than a thousand months, and whoever is deprived of its goodness is indeed deprived." (Narrated by al-Nasai, 2106; Ahmad, 8769)

"Whoever fasts Ramadan out of faith and in the hope of reward, his previous sins will be forgiven." (Bukhari 1910)

It was narrated from Sahl bin Sa'd (RA) that the Prophet (peace be upon him) said: "In Paradise there is a gate called Rayyan. On the Day of Resurrection the call will go out saying: 'Where are those who used to fast?' Whoever is among those who used to fast will enter it, and whoever enters it will never thirst again." (Sunan Ibn Majah, Book 7, Hadith 1709)

Fasting is the act of refraining from eating, drinking, and conjugal relations with one's spouse from the beginning of dawn until sunset. Fasting in Ramadan is the 3rd pillar of Islam and the 8th month of the Islamic calendar. Although fasting in the month of Ramadan is mandatory for every mature, sane Muslim, There are also other occasions where it is Sunnah to fast, as well as days on which fasting is forbidden.

Duas to open and close fast

One may read one of the following du'as when breaking the fast;

اَللّٰهُمَّ اِنِّى لَكَ صُمْتُ وَبِكَ اَمَنْتُ وَ عَلٰى رِزْقِكَ اَفْطَرْتُ

Transliteration:
Alla-hum-ma-inni-laka-sum-tu-wa-bi-ka-a-mantu-
wa-ala-riz-qi-ka af-tar-tu

Translation:
*"O Allah! I fasted for You and I believe in You and I break my
fast with what You provided."*

ذَهَبَ الظَّمَأُ وَابْتَلَّتِ الْعُرُوقُ وَثَبَتَ الْأَجْرُ إِنْ شَاءَ اللهُ

Transliteration:
Zha-ha-baz-zama-u-wab-tal-latil-u-ru-qu-
wa-tha-ba-tal-aj-ru in-sha-allah

Translation:
*"The thirst has gone and the veins are moist, and reward is
assured, if Allah
wills."*

Recommended acts during fasting

Below is a list of Prophetic (Sunnah) acts to carry out while fasting.

- To break the fast right away after sunset.

- Break your fast with dates and water.

- To consume the pre-dawn meal (Suhoor).

Disliked acts during fasting

- To complain about your hunger and thirst.

- Not to gargle water in the mouth during a shower, bath, or Wudu. This leads to water going down the throat and will potentially break your fast. When fasting, you should only rinse your mouth with water. This also applies when putting water in the nose. Putting too much water in the nose can also lead to water going up the nose and then down your throat. When fasting, it is recommended not to put too much water up the nostrils to avoid this.

- Backbiting and lying in general must be avoided. However, when fasting, the consequences are higher.

- When fasting, some people tend to spit more. This should be avoided, as this is an indecent act and further makes the world a dirty place, as many people have a habit of spitting on the floor.

Acts that break a fast

1. If one is really unwell and has to eat, drink, or take medicine, including asthma inhalers, fasting is broken if necessary for health reasons, including taking medications, eating, or drinking.

2. Anything put by force into the mouth of a fasting person (which was then swallowed).

3. Water going down the throat whilst gargling (while being conscious of one's fast):

4. To vomit a mouthful intentionally or to return vomit down the throat:

5. Intentionally swallowing a pebble, piece of paper, or any item that is not used as food or medicine: Intentionally swallowing non-food or non-medicinal items breaks the fast.

6. Swallowing something edible, equal to or bigger than a chickpea, which was stuck between the teeth. However, if it is first taken out of the mouth and swallowed, it will break the fast, whether it is smaller or bigger than the size of a chickpea. Swallowing something edible stuck between the teeth breaks the fast, whether it's removed first or not.

7. Dripping oil into the ear canal (if it goes through the ear drum): Dripping oil into the ear does not affect the fast unless it reaches the stomach through the ear drum.

8. Swallowing the blood from the gums if the colour of the blood is greater than the saliva with which it is mixed: Swallowing blood from the gums breaks the fast if its colour is greater than the saliva.

9. Kissing one's spouse and subsequently ejaculating: Ejaculation due to kissing (or any other reasons) breaks the fast, and expiation (Kaffara) is required.

10. Masturbation:

11. Engaging in sexual intercourse with one's spouse.

12. To eat and drink, forgetting that one is fasting, and thereafter thinking that the fast is broken, to eat and drink again: If one forgets they are fasting and eats or drinks, the fast remains valid once they remember and stop.

13. To eat and drink after Fajr begins or to break the fast before Maghrib due to a cloudy sky or a faulty watch, etc., and then realising one's mistake: Eating or drinking after Fajr begins or breaking the fast prematurely due to an incorrect perception of time requires immediate cessation, and the fast remains valid if the mistake is realised.

14. If a woman begins her menses during the day of Ramadan and misses every fast through menstruation: Women are exempt from fasting during menstruation, and missed fasts have to be compensated for after Ramadan.

Chapter 7

Zakaat (Almsgiving)

What is Zakaat?

Zakaat means "to increase" or "to purify." Means purifying your wealth. Zakaat should be paid by every mature and sane Muslim who meets the minimum threshold (Nisaab) with full ownership of their wealth and being in possession of that for a full lunar year. Zakaat is not required for those who are minors or insane. The minimum threshold to be eligible for Zakaat is to own enough cash and/or possessions that equate to the following:

612.36 grams of silver or 87.48 grams of . Once your wealth has reached this level and you hold it for a full year, you must pay a minimum of 2.5% of Zakaat on that wealth. For example, if you have full ownership of £100,000, whether it's a mix of cash, assets, business stock, gold, or silver, and you have held it for a full lunar year, then you will pay 2.5% of that to charity. Which will be £2,500. However, if your debts are more than your owned possessions, then you do not need to give Zakaat. If your debts are less than what you own in wealth, then this should be subtracted from your possessions.

Zakaat in the Quran

Zakaat has been mentioned 80 times in the Quran. Here are a few verses to show the importance of zakaat and the giving of charity:

وَاَقِيْمُوا الصَّلٰوةَ وَاٰتُوا الزَّكٰوةَ ؕ وَمَا تُقَدِّمُوْا لِاَنْفُسِكُمْ مِّنْ خَيْرٍ تَجِدُوْهُ عِنْدَ اللّٰهِ ؕ اِنَّ اللّٰهَ بِمَا تَعْمَلُوْنَ بَصِيْرٌ ؕ

Translation:
"Add establish the prayer and pay zakat and whatever good you send forward for yourselves you will find it with Allah. Indeed, Allah is seeing over what you do"
(Surah Baqarah, Chapter 2 : Verse 110)

اَلَّذِیْنَ یُنْفِقُوْنَ اَمْوَالَهُمْ بِالَّیْلِ وَالنَّهَارِ
سِرًّا وَّعَلَانِیَةً فَلَهُمْ اَجْرُهُمْ عِنْدَ
رَبِّهِمْ وَلَا خَوْفٌ عَلَیْهِمْ وَلَا هُمْ
یَحْزَنُوْنَ

Translation:
*"Those who spend their wealth (in the way of Allah)
by night and by day, secretly and openly, they will
have their reward with their Lord. They shall have
no fear, nor shall they grieve."*
(Surah Baqarah, Chapter 2 : Verse 274)

لَنْ تَنَالُوا الْبِرَّ حَتّٰی تُنْفِقُوْا مِمَّا تُحِبُّوْنَ
وَمَا تُنْفِقُوْا مِنْ شَیْءٍ فَاِنَّ اللهَ بِهٖ عَلِیْمٌ

Translation:
*"You can never attain virtue until you spend in Allah's cause
the things you love; and Allah is Aware of whatever you
spend."*
(Surah Al-Imran, Chapter 3 : Verse 92)

خُذْ مِنْ اَمْوَالِهِمْ صَدَقَةً تُطَهِّرُهُمْ
وَتُزَکِّیْهِمْ بِهَا وَصَلِّ عَلَیْهِمْ اِنَّ صَلٰوتَكَ
سَكَنٌ لَّهُمْ وَاللهُ سَمِیْعٌ عَلِیْمٌ

Translation:

"Oh beloved Prophet (Mohammed - peace and blessings be upon him), take the obligatory charity from their wealth, by which you may cleanse them and make them pure. Pray in their favour; indeed, your prayer is the contentment of their hearts. Allah is All-Hearing, All-Knowing."

(Surah Tawbah, Chapter 9 : Verse 103)

وَمَآ أُمِرُوٓا اِلَّا لِيَعْبُدُوا اللّٰهَ مُخْلِصِيْنَ لَهُ الدِّيْنَ حُنَفَآءَ وَيُقِيْمُوا الصَّلٰوةَ وَيُؤْتُوا الزَّكٰوةَ وَذٰلِكَ دِيْنُ الْقَيِّمَةِ ۗ

Translation:

"And they were only commanded to worship Allah, being exclusively one sided, and should establish Salaah (Prayer) and give Zakaat. And this is the right religion"

(Surah Bayyinah, Chapter 98 : Verse 5)

There is also Zakaat due on a certain number of camels, cows, sheep, goats, horses, crops, and fruits for those who own them in large numbers. However, I doubt the audience of this book will have large farms and so forth. Therefore, I will not mention these in this book. I have put this information down just to make you aware that there are laws of Zakaat on these items.

Recipients of Zakaat

Your zakat should be given to those who are poor and destitute. You can also give Zakaat to those who are in debt and to a wayfarer (someone who is stranded and/or travelling with very little resources). You cannot give Zakaat towards the operation costs or construction of a mosque. Zakaat cannot be used to shroud the deceased. Zakaat cannot be given to your father, grandfathers, son, grandsons, mother, grandmothers, granddaughters, or your wife or husband. By no means can Zakaat be given to those of the lineage of the Prophet, peace be upon him, and his bloodline exists today.

Sadaqat Al-Fitr

Sadaqat al-Fitr, or Fitrah, is mandatory for every Muslim who meets the criteria of Zakaat. This is the mandatory charity that must be given before the Eid al-Fitr prayer (the Eid after Ramadan).The Prophet peace be upon him said:

"The Messenger of Allah (peace be upon him) ordained Zakat ul Fitr [Fitrah] to purify the fasting person from indecent words or actions, and to provide food for the needy. It is accepted as Zakat for the person who gives it before the Eid prayer; but it is a mere Sadaqah for the one who gives it after the prayer."
[Collection of Abu Dawud and Ibn Majah]

The amount of Sadaqat al-Fitr that must be given as a minimum requirement is equivalent to one putting both their hands together and scooping as much flour or rice as they can. This is around £5 GBP. This is for Muslims who have an excess amount of food and must be paid before the Eid Al-Fitr prayer. Preferably, one should pay this towards the end of Ramadan, so the money reaches the poor before the Eid prayer, which they can utilise. The requirements for who can and cannot receive this are the same for Zakaat.

Chapter 8

Hajj
(Pilgrimage)

The 4th pillar of Islam is Hajj (mandatory pilgrimage). In the lifetime of a Muslim it is mandatory that they complete the Hajj at least once. However you must fit the two criteria's below.

- Having the financial means
- Strong health (due to the tough physical efforts needed).

"And Hajj (pilgrimage to Makkah) to the House (Ka'bah) is a duty that mankind owes to Allah, those who can afford the expenses (for one's conveyance, provision and residence); and whoever disbelieves [i.e. denies Hajj (pilgrimage to Makkah), then he is a disbeliever of Allah], then Allah stands not in need of any of the 'Alamin (mankind, jinn and all that exists)." [Al-Imran 3:97]

Abu Hurayrah (may Allah be pleased with him) said: I heard the Messenger of Allah (peace and blessings of Allah be upon him) say: "Whoever performs Hajj and does not utter obscenities or commit sin, will come back as on the day when his mother bore him." (Narrated by al-Bukhari, 1521; Muslim, 1350)

History of Hajj

The first rituals of Hajj were bestowed upon Prophet Ibrahim (Abraham). Peace be upon him by Allah. Prophet Ibrahim (Abraham) and his son Prophet Ismaeel (Ishmael), peace be upon them, were given the honour to build the Kabah (house of God). Prophet Ibrahim, peace be upon him, would perform Hajj every year after the construction of the Kabah. After his departure from the world, this would continue through his children. However, over time, after generations, The Kabah became the pinnacle point of idol worshipping. People would place their idols in and around the Kabah and worship them instead of the one God. People started to perform Tawaf (circulation) of the Kabah naked. They believed they should present themselves to their lord (or lords, as there were many statues) in their natural born form. Until the Prophet, peace be upon him, conquered Makkah, these were the acts taking place around the house of God.

The acts of Hajj are mainly in remembrance of the life of Hazrat[1] Ibrahim and his family; peace be upon them. For example, the stoning of the devil

---

[1] Hazrat = A respectful title given to those close to Allah

during Hajj is to commemorate the time when Satan appeared before Hazrat Ibrahim, peace be upon him, trying to tempt him, and he rejected his advances by throwing stones at him on numerous occasions. The walking and running between Mount Safa and Marwa reminds me of when the wife of Prophet Ibrahim's wife, Hazrat Haja, peace be upon them, was running between these two destinations in search of water in the desert. Then, by the mercy of Allah, the ZamZam water was given to her. During Hajj, it is mandatory for Muslims around the world to sacrifice a goat as a minimum requirement, to relive and experience the sacrifice of Prophet Ibrahim, peace be upon him, who was going to sacrifice his son, Prophet Ismaeel, peace be upon him, as this is what God showed him in a dream. As this was the order of Allah, he didn't hesitate; when it came to sacrificing his son, the knife wouldn't cut through the neck of Prophet Ismaeel (Ishmael). Peace be upon him. This was a test from Allah to Prophet Ibrahim, peace be upon him, to see if he was willing to sacrifice his son. The purpose of sacrificing an animal during Hajj (known as Qurbaani) is a test from Allah to see who are firm Muslims. Who are willing to sacrifice an animal so those who are in less fortunate positions can be joyful on Eid Al-Adha and eat meat, which may be scarce for them? The benefit this has for Muslims is that it strengthens their faith. You are admitting to Allah the wrongs you have done in life, and may a sacrifice be somewhat of a compensation. Allah says: It is neither their meat nor their blood that reaches allah; it is your piety that reaches him. (surah al-hajj, chapter 22—hajj: verse 37).

Acts of Hajj

1. Tawaf (circumambulation): This is when you go around the Kaba seven times.

2. Sa'ee: walking and jogging between the mountains of Safa and Marwah.

3. Staying in Mina on 8th Dhil-Hijjah.

4. To stay in Aarafah on the 9th of Dhil-Hijjah.

5. Staying the night in Muzdalifah on 9th Dhil-Hijjah.

6. To stone Jamarat Al-Aqab. On the 10th of Dhil-Hijjah in Mina.

7. Sacrifice (Qurbaani) a minimum of a sheep or ram in Mina.

8. Shaving or trimming the hair on the head. It is Sunnah for men to shave their entire heads. It is farad (mandatory) to cut a small piece of hair at least. To maximise the reward, men should shave the entire head. Women must cut at least 2 inches of hair.

9. Tawaf-Al-Ifadah: to perform Tawaf (circulation of the Kabah) and then to perform Sa'ee (walking and jogging in between Mount Safa and Marwa).

10. Stoning the three pliiars in Mina. This takes place on the 11th and 12th of Dhil-Hijjah.

11. Farewell Tawaf. Also known as (Tawaf Al-Wada). Performing the final Tawaf (cultivation) of the Kabah.

(1) Begin by performing a 2 Rakat Nafl Salah at the Miqat (this is the boundary where one must enter the state of Ihram), then proceed to make Ihram specifically for Hajj.

(2) During Ihram, strictly abstain from all prohibited actions (Haraam).

(3) Maintain a profound respect and sanctity for the Baitullah Shareef (Kabah) in your heart while reciting the Talbiyah throughout the journey towards the Makkah Shareef.

(4) Enter the Masjid with your right foot and, upon entering, recite the Du'a for entering.

(5) Upon entering Masjid-al-Haram, raise your hands and recite Takbeer and Tahleel upon seeing the Holy Ka'bah. There is a narrated Du'a by Prophet Muhammad (Peace be upon him) for increasing the sanctity of the Ka'bah.

(6) Make the intention before beginning Tawaf.

(7). Commence Tawaf-e-Qudum (the first Tawaf) immediately after entering Masjid-al-Haram.

(8) Start Tawaf aligned with the Hajar-e-Aswad (the Black Stone).

(9) At the beginning of Tawaf, if possible, kiss the Black Stone.

(10) If kissing the Black Stone is not feasible, indicate by raising both hands and pointing both palms towards the Hajar-e-Aswad, saying Takbeer.

(11) Practice Idtiba (keeping the right shoulder uncovered) and Ramal in the first 3 rounds of Tawaf.

(12) Upon completing Tawaf, perform 2 Rakat Wajib-ut-Tawaf Salah behind the Maqam-e-Ibrahim if possible. Otherwise, perform it anywhere in Masjid al-Haram.

(13) Drink the Holy Zam Zam water while standing and facing the Holy Ka'bah.

(14) After completing Salah, if possible, kiss the Black Stone, then proceed to Mount Safa.

(15) Read the specified verse in hope of gaining goodness from Mount Safa and also recite, "I start in the way Allah commanded us to start." (Surah Baqarah, Verse 158)

(16) Perform Sa'ee (walking and running) between Safa and Marwa, completing 7 rounds.

(17) If possible, perform 2 Rakat Nafl Salah in Masjid al-Haram.

(18) Maintain the state of Ihram and avoid becoming Halaal. No trimming or shaving of hair is allowed.

(19) Stay in Makkah-al-Mukarramah, constantly reciting the Talbiyah and engaging in numerous Nafl prayers.

(20) On the 8th Zil-Hijjah, head to Mina, perform Zuhr, Asr, Maghrib, and Isha Salah, and stay the night.

(21) On the 9th Zil-Hijjah, perform Fajr Salah at Mina and then head to Arafah after sunrise.

(22) At Arafah, go to Masjid-e-Namira, listen to the Imam's Khutbah, and perform Zuhr and Asr Salah together. Otherwise, pray for them at their proper times.

(23) Immediately after completing Salah and other necessities,.

(24) Stay at Arafah until sunset on the 9th Zil-Hijjah.

(25) After sunset on the 9th Zil-Hijjah, head to Muzdalifah from Arafah without performing Maghrib Salah.

(26) Upon arriving at Muzdalifah, pray both Maghrib and Isha Salah together at Isha time, then spend the night there.

(27) On the 10th Zil-Hijjah, perform Fajr Salah early at Muzdalifah. After sunrise, stay briefly, and then head to Mina.

(28) Upon reaching Mina on the 10th Zil-Hijjah, pelt stones at Jamara-e-Aqabah, fulfil Dam-as-Shukr, and shave or cut hair to become Halaal.

(29) After becoming Halaal, go to Makkah-al-Mukarramah and perform Tawaf-e-Ziyarah.

(30) After completing Tawaf-e-Ziyarah, return to Mina and stay there.

(31) On the 11th Zil-Hijjah, pelt all 3 Jamaraat with 7 stones each.

(32) On the 12th Zil-Hijjah, again pelt all 3 Jamaraat with 7 stones each, then head to Makkah Sharif.

(33) If staying at Mina on the night of the 12th Zil-Hijjah, repeat the stoning on the 13th Zil-Hijjah.

(34) En route from Mina to Makkah, briefly stop at Muhassab.

(35) Before leaving Makkah Sharif, perform the Farewell Tawaf (Tawaf-e-Wida).

Although the acts of Hajj are all based in Makkah. After the days Hajj you should attend to Madinah-Tul-Munawwaarah for visit (Ziyarah) of the Prophet peace be upon him, the Ahlul-Bayt and Sahaba (Companions of the prophet peace be upon him).

عَنْ اَبِيْ هُرَيْرَةَ رَضِيَ اللهُ عَنْهُ اَنَّ رَسُوْلَ اللهِ صَلَّى اللهُ عَلَيْهِ وَ سَلَّمَ قَالَ اِنَّ الْإِيْمَانَ لَيَأْرِزُ إِلَى الْمَدِيْنَةِ كَمَا تَأْرِزُ الْحَيَّةُ اِلَى حُجْرِهَا (مسلم)

Translation:

Abu Hurairah (*RadiyAllahu Anhu*) narrates that indeed Rasoolullah (Peace be upon him)) said: "Indeed Imaan (belief) receives shelter when it reaches Madinah just like a snake getting shelter from its hole." (Sahih Muslim)

عَنْ عَبْدِ اللهِ بْنِ عُمَرَ رَضِيَ اللهُ عَنْهُمَا قَالَ رَسُوْلَ اللهِ صَلَّى اللهُ عَلَيْهِ وَ سَلَّمَ مَنْ حَجَّ الْبَيْتَ وَ لَمْ يَزُرْنِيْ فَقَدْ جَفَانِيْ

(رواه ابن عدي بسند جيد حسن)

Translation:

Abdullah ibn Umar (*RadiyAllahu Anhuma*) narrates that Rasoolullah (Peace be upon him)) said: "Whoever does Hajj of the Holy Ka'bah and doesn't visit me it is as if he harmed me." (Ibn 'Adi - with a good and Hasan chain)

عَنْ أَنَسِ بْنِ مَالِكٍ رَضِيَ اللهُ عَنْهُ قَالَ قَالَ رَسُوْلُ اللهِ صَلَّى اللهُ عَلَيْهِ وَ سَلَّمَ مَنْ زَارَنِيْ بِالْمَدِيْنَةِ مُحْتَسِبًا كُنْتُ لَهُ شَهِيْدًا وَ شَفِيْعًا يَوْمَ الْقِيَامَةِ

Translation:

Anas ibn Malik (*RadiyAllahu Anhu*) narrates that Rasoolullah (Peace be upon him)) said: "Whoever visits Madinah to visit only me, I will be a witness for him and intercede for him on the day of judgement." (Ash-Shafaa lil-Qadee 321, Al-Jami' as-Sagheer 8716 – Imam Suyuti said this chain is Hasan).

When embarking on a journey from Hajj or Umrah towards Madinah Shareef, one should set the sincere and exclusive intention of being in the presence of Sayyidina Rasoolullah (Peace be upon him), recognizing it as a crucial criterion for success. In addition to the Ziyarah of the blessed Rawda (tomb) of Rasoolullah (Peace be upon him), one should also intend to perform Salah in Masjid-e-Nabawi to attain the satisfaction of Allah. The encouragement for praying Salah in Masjid-e-Nabawi comes directly from Rasoolullah (Peace be upon him) himself.

As narrated by Abu Hurairah (RadiyAllahu Anhu), Prophet Muhammad (Peace be upon him) stated: "Praying one Rakat in this mosque (Masjid-e-Nabawi) is better than 1000 Rakats of prayer in other mosques except Masjid-al-Haram." (Bukhari No. 1190) Another narration in Ibn Majah mentions Rasoolullah (Peace be upon him) saying: "Praying one Rakat in Masjid-e-Nabawi is better than praying 50,000 Rakats in any other Mosque of the world."

Here are some guidelines for your visit to Madinah Shareef:

- Engage in excessive Durood and Salaam during your journey to Ziyarah.

- Increase the number of Durood and Salaam as you approach Madinah Shareef, and pray to Allah for the acceptance of your actions.

- Before entering Madinah, perform ghusl and wear clean clothes if possible. Maintain the status and respect of Madinah in your heart.

- Upon reaching the borders of the city, intensify your recitation of Durood and Salaam, elevating your emotional state.

- Upon entering Madinah, leave your luggage in your accommodation, and if possible, take a shower or perform Wudhu. Walk towards Masjid-e-Nabawi with respect and courtesy.

- Enter the Masjid with your right foot, recite Durood and Salaam, and then perform 2 Rakat Tahiyyat-ul-Masjid in Riyad-ul-Jannah or any other part of the Masjid if it is not during a Makrooh time.

- After finishing the prayer, recite Durood, Salaam, and any dua of your choice.

- Proceed to give Salaam (peace) upon the Prophet; peace be upon him with love and affection in your heart. Stand respectfully in front of the Rawdha Sharif (the tomb of the Prophet, peace be upon him) and offer your Salaam.

- If friends and family request, convey their Salaam to the Prophet, peace be upon him, after giving your own Salaam.

- Through the medium of the Prophet, peace be upon him, make dua to Allah for all your beneficial wishes.

- Standing in the presence of the Prophet, peace be upon him, and offering abundant Durood and Salaam is a highly rewarding act. Stand before the Rawdah Mubarak, if possible, and offer copious amounts of durood and Salaam (salutations and peace), seeking his intercession without causing inconvenience to others.

- Conclude by offering Salaam to the caliphs of Sayyindina Abu Bakr Siddique (RadiyAllahu Anhu) and Ameer-ul-Mumineen, Sayyindina Umar Farooq (RadiyAllahu Anhu), each located approximately one arm's length from the Prophet's resting place.

Chapter 9
Seerah

Life of the Prophet Muhammad peace be upon him

Before the birth of the Prophet (peace be upon him)

Before the Prophet's birth, peace be upon him. The world was in a severely dark place. As there was a 570-year gap between the time of Prophet Isa (Jesus) (peace be upon him), people had long lost the original tradition of Christianity. In many places around the world, people were worshipping the sea, the moon, the stars, the sun, Jinns, and some even worshipped fire (Zoroastrians).

The economic system was fairly poor in most parts of the world, and society was divided into groups depending on one's personal level of wealth. There was no equality between the rich and poor. Most parts of the world suffer from immoral social acts. For example, the practice of incest was widely spread in places like Iran and among Zoroastrians. In India, women had close to zero rights. They had to obey their husbands at all times without having their own opinion. In India, regardless of how young the woman was, if her husband had died, then it was seen as a highly appreciated practice to burn herself along with the corpse of her husband. If she didn't have the courage for this, she was not allowed to get married again, nor was she allowed to adorn herself with good clothes or jewellery.

Living in the modern world, where we see the mass media slander Islam and generalise us for all the negative things you can think of, It's important to know that it was through the Prophet Muhammad, peace be upon him, that the world went through a purification process. Prior to the blessed birth of the Prophet, peace be upon him, the Arabs had adopted cruel acts. For example, having a daughter was seen as bad luck. Therefore, Arabs buried their daughters at birth. The connotation was that she may be "evil" as she turns into a woman. Meaning she might end up in prostitution or something similar of that nature. In many parts of the world, marriage doesn't really exist. There were many "contractual marriages." Such as time-limited marriages, known as mu'tah, which unfortunately is still present in this day and age amongst the Shia community. This is where both parties (the family of the man and woman) get married, for either an hour, a day, a week, or maybe a month or year. Just to satisfy their sexual desires. Once the agreement of time is finished, both parties part ways. Other marriages, such as two men swapping wives, were common. Brothel houses would have flags above the house, signifying that a particular house was there for those indecent acts. This, of course, resulted in many pregnancies where the father was mostly unknown and no care or responsibility was taken for the woman or baby.

Another form of marriage that existed was that a man would marry his daughter to another man in return for marrying that man's own daughter.

Extreme usage of alcohol was common, even in Arabia. Idol worship was their main religion. The irony is that many idols would be kept in the Kabah for people to visit.

Although this is a short description of the global circumstances that were customs prior to the Prophet's birth, peace be upon him. For a more detailed analysis, please refer to Volume 1 of Zia-Un-Nabi by Pir Karam Shah (Al-Azhari P. K., 2013)

Before the birth of the Prophet, peace be upon him, in the same year (570 AD), The king of Yemen, Abraha, was jealous that Arabs visited Makkah in large numbers. He tried to boycott people from visiting the Kabah. The Kabah prior to the birth of the Prophet, peace be upon him, had a total of 360 idols inside it, which people used to come and visit. Due to the jealousy Abraha had of people visiting the Kabah, He decided to launch an attack to break the Kabah down. At that time, the leader of the Quraysh tribe was the grandfather of the Prophet, peace be upon him (Abdul Muttalib). He ordered the people of Makkah to evacuate the area and seek shelter elsewhere. On the day of the attack, the people of Makkah could see the large army and elephants that Abraha had ordered to make the attack. The people of Makkah were left hopeless. However, as previously stated, The people of Quraysh were noble and did not participate in evil as many other Arabs did. Such as drinking alcohol, burying the daughters alive, or worshipping idols. They firmly believed that there was only one God. Abdul Muttalib prayed to Allah for protection against this unjust act that Abraha was committing. As the army and numerous elephants marched towards the Kabah, Birds from the sky threw pebbles at the army and elephants, and they would instantly die. The king of Yemen, Abraha, also died during the incident, and his plan failed. This is mentioned in the Qurah in the chapter "Al-Feel," chapter/Surah number 104.

The birth of the Prophet (peace be upon him)

The prophet, peace be upon him, was born at the time of Fajr on Monday, during the Arabic month of Rabi-Ul-Awwal. Most scholars say he was born on the 12th of Rabi-Ul-Awwal. (which corresponds to August 20, 570 AD) However, the exact date of Rabi-Ul-Awwal is not known. But what is definitely certain is that he was born in the month of Rabi-Ul-Awwal on a

Monday in the year 570 AD. The Prophet, peace be upon him, was born in Makkah, near Masjid al-Haram. Currently, the exact same place of the birth of the Prophet Muhammad, peace be upon him, has now been turned into an Islamic library.

Numerous miracles took place at the time the Prophet, peace be upon him, was born. A light came out of his mother, Aminah, that lit up the palaces of Syria. The idols that were kept in the kabah all fell down. A star was born in the sky. A scholar of the Jewish religion of the time was living in Makkah. At the time of the Prophet's birth, the Jewish scholar looked into the sky and saw a star, which indicated the final Prophet had been born. He then asked the tribe of Quraysh if a baby had been born, to which they replied that Abdul Muttalib (the grandfather of the Prophet, peace be upon him) had a grandson that was born. 14 towers of the palace in Iran had fallen, and a fire that had been burning for centuries in the fire temple of Iran was suddenly put out when the Prophet, peace be upon him, was born.

Another miracle is that when Aminah (the mother of the prophet Muhammad, peace be upon him) was in her pregnancy, she felt no hardship during the entire time she was carrying the beloved Prophet, peace be upon him. Most traditions state that the Prophet was born circumcised (this is mandatory for all males in Islam and should take place within the first month of the baby being born) and that he was also born with a veil around his waist to cover his body parts. This in itself is a miracle, as God is respecting his beloved Prophet, peace be upon him, so no one can look at his body parts.

The Prophet Muhammad, peace be upon him, belongs to the Quraysh tribe. The people of Quraysh were known to have good character. They were generous to others and are known to be the most honest of people. Prior to the birth of the Prophet, peace be upon him, there was no monarch or government that controlled Arabia. Rather, they had various tribes, each made up of multiple families. For example, the Banu-Hashim family (which is the family that the Prophet peace be upon him belongs to) was part of the Quraysh tribe. A unique attribute of the Quraysh tribe was that it was their responsibility to look after the Kabah (House of God). They would further take care of the pilgrims during their visits. The Quraysh were among the most noble tribes, as they descend from Prophet Ibrahim (Abraham). Peace be upon them. When the Prophet peace be upon him was born, his grandfather Abdul Muttalib prepared a large feast in Makkah, which was attended by the Quraysh.

Meaning of the name Muhammad

The name Muhammad means "the all-praised."

Childhood of the Prophet Muhammad (peace be upon him)

The Prophet's father (peace be upon him) passed away before the birth of the final prophet. He had various milk mothers while in infancy and throughout his early years. It was custom in the lands of Arabia to send children at a young age to the desert to live with wet nurses. This is for various reasons. One of the reasons was that this was a great way to become fluent in the Arabic language. The desert life was much healthier than the towns and cities. This lifestyle of being raised in the desert also made children humble, as they weren't surrounded by luxuries. From a young age, they would be taught to work hard in order to earn a living as well as develop a positive character. The mother of the Prophet, peace be upon him, Hazrat Aminah, was cautious if someone would accept her son, as her husband passed away before the birth of the Prophet, peace be upon him, and the financial conditions were not the best as they were relying on the Prophet's grandfather, Hazrat Abdul Muttalib, to take care of them.

Sayyida[2] Halima arrived in Makkah with her husband to look for a child to take back to the desert that they could nurture. At that time, Sayyida Halima and her husband were not really financially stable, plus she looked quite weak. No other mothers gave their children to her to take back to the desert. However, as she was eager to take a child back and saw the Prophet, peace be upon him, The Prophet peace be upon him's mother could see that she was a loving and caring person and was happy to send the Prophet peace be upon him with her.

After taking the Prophet, peace be upon him, into their care with the rest of their family, Allah sent them numerous blessings. The animals they kept for grazing were getting stronger and healthier. As did Sayyida Halima. Their financial condition improved significantly, and the family loved and

---

[2] Sayyida is the title used when a female is a family member/descendant of the Prophet peace be upon him. For males, the term "Sayyid" is used.

took care of the Prophet, peace be upon him, like he was their own child. When the Prophet peace be upon him was two years old, he went with Sayyida Halima to visit his mother, Sayyida Aminah. His mother was pleased to see that the Prophet, peace be upon him, had become healthy and strong. After this short stay, his mother sent him back to the desert with Sayyida Halima.

Even during the Prophet's childhood, the other children would notice the extraordinary behaviour of his surroundings. For example, stones give the message of greetings to the Prophet, peace be upon him. During his time in the desert, people also witnessed when Jibreel (Angel Gabriel), peace be upon him, came and cut open the chest of the Prophet, peace be upon him, and washed his heart with Zamzam water in a golden basin. From his childhood, people knew that he was something special. Wherever he went, he blessed the households of their people, their livelihood, their stock, and so forth.

When the Prophet peace be upon him was six years old, Sayyida Halima returned him to his mother, Sayyida Aminah.

Sayyida Aminah visited the grave of her husband Abdullah in Madinah. The journey from Makkah to Madinal is approximately 280 miles away. Obviously, back in those days, they either walked, rode camels, donkeys, or horses as their means of travel. She set off with the Prophet, peace be upon him, her farther-in-law, Abdul Muttalib, and one of her servants, Umm Ayman. They spent around one month in Madinah. During the return of the journey, Sayyida Aminah became ill and passed away.

After this incident, the Prophet, peace be upon him, was in the full care of his grandfather, Abdul Muttalib. Abdul Muttalib loved the Prophet, peace be upon him, more than his own children and knew that one day he would hold a strong position in society. When the Prophet, peace be upon him, was 8 years old, The grandfather who loved him and took him under his care sadly passed away.

This is a crucial point to make here. We must think deeply about the mental and spiritual effects this would have on a normal person. If a child was born and their father passed away before their birth, and then their mother passed away at a young age, so did their grandfather. Imagine what that child must be going through. Constantly moving from house to house to be taken care of. Not having much of a father figure around, not having the joyful childhood most people have. For most, this is a traumatic experience. All this happened when the Prophet, peace be upon him, was just 8 years old. Yet, he still rose above all the difficulties; he became the best leader the world has ever seen. He gave rights to everyone, regardless of their power, wealth, and social status. He cared for orphans and those who were most vulnerable. He reformed society and brought the world into light after centuries of darkness. We must reflect on our own lives. Our difficulty, compared to the difficulty of the Prophets, is not even a taste of what they had to experience. Yet we are surrounded by all the luxuries of the world, and most people are still unhappy with their lives.

After the passing of Hazrat Abdul Muttalib, The prophet, peace be upon him, was taken into the care of his paternal uncle, Hazrat Abu Talib. He also took great care of his nephew and had a stronger preference for the Prophet, peace be upon him, than his own children, just like Abdul Muttalib. Many are under the perception that the Prophet, peace be upon him, was always financially poor. This is not the case. His uncle, Hazrat Abu Talib, was a wealthy entrepreneur. To the extent that they had maids and personal tailors for their clothing, How rich does someone have to be in this day and age to have their own tailor and multiple maids? The Prophet, peace be upon him, after the age of 8 grew up around wealth, but due to his humility for the poor. He wanted to spend his life resembling them. We will later talk about his own business ventures when he was an adult.

At the age of 12, the Prophet, peace be upon him, went on his first business trip with his uncle, Hazrat Abu Talib, to Syria. When they reached an area called Busra, they met Bahira, the monk. According to some, his real name was Georges. The monk recognised that the young boy at the time was the final messenger to arrive. Bahira was, of course, a genuine monk, a man of spirituality for his time. He took the hand of the Prophet, peace be upon him, and said he would be the master for all humans and that Allah would send him a message that would be a mercy to all of mankind. When Abu Talib replied, the monk knew this. The monk said that when they were appearing from this direction, the stones and trees prostrated themselves. Bahira the monk also recognised the seal of Prophethood, which was below the left shoulder of the Prophet, peace be upon him. It was under the influence and recommendation of the monk that Hazrat Abu Talib sent the Prophet Muhammad, peace be upon him, back to Makkah and didn't let him progress with the journey to Syria due to the fear of the Jews, and that if they found out he was the last Prophet, then they certainly would've killed him.

The Prophet Muhammad (peace be upon him) & Sayyida Khadijah

A business proposal had come to the Prophet, peace be upon him, from Hazrat Khadijah. The Prophet, peace be upon him, was known to people due to his trustworthiness and honesty. At this time, Hazrat Khadijah Bint Khuwaylid was a widow. She was also one of the most successful female business figures during this period in Makkah. The current media tends to give a negative representation of women in Islam as being apparently "oppressed," that they only have to obey their husbands, dress modestly, and that's their life. This is the beauty of Islam. Women have the power in our religion to go and provide for themselves if need be. In the western world, such as the USA and UK, women were only allowed to vote politically in the 20th century, which is still quite recent. Women are still having to fight western corporations for equal pay across all spectrums in the hierarchy. Islam bought equality for men and women when it comes to earning a living and being part of society.

Hazrat Khadijah came to an agreement with the Prophet, peace be upon him. If he was able to go to Syria and sell all her stock, she would give him a share of the profit. Which he, peace be upon him, happily agreed to. This was the second business trip to Syria for the Prophet, peace be upon him. He managed to sell the stock at higher profits than expected due to his honesty, which pleased Hazrat Khadijah. Businesses nowadays talk about customer service and customer satisfaction. All these skills derive from Islam. The Prophet, peace be upon him, was the most skilled person, regardless of which department you put him in. Entrepreneurship is a Sunnah of the Prophet (peace be upon him and other Prophets), which we need to try to revive. In most cases, working for yourself is the best way to develop as a Muslim and in your everyday life. The situation is worse when it comes to Jummah, where you may need an hour or two off from work. What about all the religious nights that are strongly encouraged for Muslims to stay awake and seek forgiveness from Allah? Such as the 15th of Sha'baan (Night of Baraat/Laylatul-Baraat). The last 10 nights of Ramadan, the nightfall before Eid, and many more? How many employers in the modern world will you give you these times off? As Muslims, we believe that our real struggle is to work for the hereafter. If we can't utilise these holy days and nights in our youth, when we have the energy and strength to worship a lot, then what hope do you have if and when we become old? How do we not know that we may fall into a sickness that makes us weak? It can even happen at a young age. Muslims are always having to battle between faith and corporate life. We should take a step back and think about unique opportunities to capitalise on. Not only to make a living for ourselves, but to further have the disposable income to support our Islamic communities. Such as donating towards Islamic projects, places of worship, or places of Islamic studies. It can even be to serve the community by having your own charity, to feed homeless people in your area, or to provide shelter for those in need. Hazrat Khadijah further used her wealth after marrying the Prophet, peace be upon him, to promote the Islamic movement.

The marriage between the Prophet (peace be upon him) & Sayyida Khadijah

Before we go into marriage, We need to understand the variance of both the Prophet Muhammad's (peace be upon him) background and that of Hazrat Khadijah. The Prophet, peace be upon him, came from a much less strong financial background compared to Hazrat Khadijah. As a young boy, he aided his uncle Abu Talib and worked as a shepard. Whereas, Hazrat Khadijah came from a background of wealth. Something that is extremely rare in this day and age. How many people do you know where the wife is richer than the husband? The ratio will most likely be very low compared to the people you know where the man is richer than the wife, right? This goes to show that wealth is not needed for a successful marriage. Prior to this marriage, Hazrat Khadijah had already been married twice, with both of her husband's passing away, leaving both their children with her.

Prior to the marriage. Hazrat Khadijah sent a close friend, Nufaysah Bint Munyah, to get an opinion on his personality and if he wanted to get married or not. The Prophet, peace be upon him, didn't want to get married at the time due to his financial situation. Nufaysah then told him not to worry about that and that Nufaysah would take the responsibility. The Prophet, peace be upon him, then asked who she was on behalf of. To which she replied, Khadijah. The Prophet, peace be upon him, then sent his uncle Hazrat Abu Talib to send a proposal. Which was then obviously mutually agreed.

The Prophet peace be upon him was 25 at the time when he married Hazrat Khadijah, and she was 40 (this is differed upon). Together, they had six children. 4 daughters and 2 sons. The list is given below.

1. Umm Kulthum
2. Ruqayah
3. Fatima
4. Zainab
5. Abdullah
6. Qasim

Hazrat Khadijah played a crucial role in the life of the Prophet, peace be upon him. She was the first to accept Islam; she gave him encouragement and comfort when everyone else had turned away from him. The Prophet's love for her was something unique, as he didn't marry anyone else until she passed away. She passed away at age 65. The sons of the Prophet, peace be upon him (including his other wives), all passed away during childhood. One of the reasons for this is that they would've had to carry on the legacy of their father's Prophethood if they reached the age of maturity. This is something that is not possible, as the Prophet Muhammad, peace be upon him, is the final messenger.

Reconstruction of the Kabah

When the Prophet peace be upon him was 35, A reconstruction of the Kabah took place under the decision of the leaders of Quraysh. This led to the size of the Kabah increasing as its walls were raised and any damages that had appeared on the Kabah were refurbished. Most of these damages were due to heavy rain falling in Makkah, and there wasn't much of a roof during these times. The black stone (Al-Hajar Al-Aswad) was also to be refitted back into the Kabah. This caused quite a big uproar amongst the tribes, as it was seen as an act of honour, to which tribe will refit the black stone in its corner. The disunity that this caused almost started a war in Makkah. Around 40 days had passed without a resolution. One of the elderly men said that they should wait until the next morning, and the first person to walk through the gate of the Haram (a sacred place) will give their verdict on the matter. When the people of Makkah saw that the first person to walk through the gate was the Prophet, peace be upon him, They rejoiced as they knew that the Prophet, peace be upon him, was a fair man. Some even started to shout at this moment, "Al-Ameen is here." meaning trustworthy. The Prophet, peace be upon him, then took off his robe or cloak and placed the black stone in the middle of the garment. He then got each leader of the tribes to hold a certain part of the robe or cloak and place the black stone back in the corner of the Kabah together. As a result of this gesture, they all felt honoured. Further friction and the start of a war were avoided by this action of the Prophet, peace be upon him.

Revelation

Now 40 years old. The Prophet, peace be upon him, received his first revelation. The Prophet, peace be upon him, would spend a lot of his time in seclusion up in the mountains. He would spend his secluded time at Mount Noor (Jabal-e-Noor); on the peak of that mountain lies a cave known as "Hira" (Ghar-e-Hira). He would spend his time in meditation and contemplation. Back in that era, there were no skyscrapers or government-funded clock towers like they have now. From the mountain, you were able to have a direct view of the Kabah. Masjid-Al-Haram (in Makkah) to Jabal-e-Noor is around 6 miles away. Nowadays, we can get in a car and be at either of these destinations within 20 or 25 minutes. Back then, the Prophet, peace be upon him, would either walk or ride horse, mule, or camel to the destination in the blazing Arabian heat. Consuming much more time than it does today. On top of that, climbing the mountain today would take around 3–4 hours for the average person. Today, the government has implemented a staircase going all the way to the peak of the mountain. Even around 100 or 200 years ago, there was no staircase. Only the healthiest of people would manage to climb to the top without any safety equipment. We should reflect on the efforts our predecessors made to visit these holy sites and how fortunate we are today to have easy access to them. Imagine how long the climb would take for the Prophet, peace be upon him. He, peace be upon him, would spend days or weeks, sometimes even months on end, up the mountain. Hazrat Khadijah would travel from their house to the top of the mountain to take food and water for him. Those who have been to Hajj or Umrah will surely be able to taste the slightest bit of sacrifice that was made in order to establish Islam. Carrying yourself to the top of the mountain is hard enough, let alone carrying food and water with you. That is enough to last a few days at least, like Hazrat Khadijah did.

On a night in the month of Ramadan. The angel Gabriel (Jibraeel) came to the Prophet, peace be upon him, while on Jabal-e-Noor to reveal the first verses of the Quran. The angel Jibraeel told the Prophet, peace be upon him, to read. Which he replied, "I am not a reader." Jibraeel, peace be upon him, then pressed himself against the Prophet, peace be upon him, and told him to read again. The Prophet then repeated that he is not a reader. This happened a couple of times until the Prophet, peace be upon him, recited the verses of revelation from God. Which is in Surah A'laq (Chapter 96 in the Quran). This chapter has a total of 19 verses. During the first revelation, Only the first five verses were revealed. After this incident occurred, The Prophet, peace be upon him, went home and sought comfort from his wife, as this was an unusual experience for him.

Although the first revelation came to the Prophet, peace be upon him, aged 40, It does not mean that he became a prophet at age 40. He was already a prophet before he was born. The Prophet, peace be upon him, said that he was a prophet when Adam, peace be upon him, was in between soul and body (this hadith can be found in the collection of Tirmizi). Meaning that the Prophet Muhammad, peace be upon him, was a prophet before Allah created Prophet Adam, peace be upon him. Unfortunately, even Muslims are under the misconception that the Prophet was only a prophet after the age of 40. This is totally wrong and an immoral type of thinking towards the Prophet Muhammad, peace be upon him. If Allah were to send down a prophet, then he obviously knows the best time to send a prophet to guide mankind. It's not as if prophets were sent, then God thought to himself, "Oh, he'll make a good prophet; I'll just choose him." This way of thinking is baseless and doesn't make logical sense.

There is wisdom in why the Prophet, peace be upon him, remained silent about his Prophethood to his community prior to 40. He had to get to know his community and what he's surrounded by. During the first 40 years, he carefully analysed the situations around him and what he could face when declaring his Prophethood to the masses. It's like a new neighbour moving into the community that nobody knows. It will take time to get to know the person, their family, what their personality is like, and so on.

The start of the Islamic movement

After the declaration of Prophethood, Prophet Muhammad, peace be upon him, started to invite family and close friends first to Islam, as they knew him better than anyone else in Makkah and knew he was an honest man. Thus leading to their accepting Islam. The first child to accept Islam was Hazrat Ali. Who later became the 4th caliph of Islam. Shortly after followed the acceptance of the 1st caliph of Islam. Hazrat Abu Bakr Siddique. Hazrat Abu Bakr was a successful and honest businessman who would often free slaves due to their mistreatment. He was brave and wasn't afraid to stand up for his beliefs in Allah and the final messenger. Through his influence, many others accepted Islam. Even before the establishment of Prophethood, Hazrat Abu Bakr didn't participate in idol worshipping, consume alcohol, or gamble like many others did during the days of ignorance.

During the first three years of declared Prophethood, Islamic preaching remained secretive due to the circumstances in society. The majority of the world has been worshipping elements and idols, and to snap out of that habit takes a lot of time. The wisdom in the first three years of Prophethood was to try to gain as many followers as possible and to turn people back to the one God. This is a message that many would not take lightly, as they had been practicing false God's for a long time. Over these three years, revelation kept coming to the Prophet, peace be upon him, from Allah through the angel Jibraeel (Gabriel).

Over time, when word started getting out that the Prophet Muhammad, peace be upon him, was preaching an entirely new religion, the people of Makkah started to raise concerns. The Quraysh were particularly worried that their idols would not be worshipped. Which means the pilgrims that come from around the world to worship Idols may be influenced by the teachings of the Prophet, peace be upon him, thus leading to financial loss for tribes like the Quraysh. This led to tribes trying to bribe the Prophet, peace be upon him, with enough money to make him rich for his entire life, but he strongly refused. As the land of Arabia had no governing law, people were free to do whatever they liked. Leaders of the Quraysh would start a mass torturing spree for anyone who excepted the words of the Prophet, peace be upon him, and who believed in one God and the final messenger.

Among those who were tortured by the people of Makkah was Hazrat Bilal. He was known to be the caller to prayer (Mua'zzin) during the time of the Prophet, peace be upon him. He would have a rope around his neck and be dragged along the streets of Makkah. He was further made to lay on his back on the hot Arabian sand and have a rock placed on his chest and stomach while being whipped by his owner, as he was a slave and had accepted the message of Islam. During this beating, they tried to make Hazrat Bilal denounce his faith in Islam. However, he kept true to his word and kept repeating that there is only one God. While the beating of Hazrat Bilal was intensifying, the news of this event reached the Prophet, peace be upon him. Who sent Hazrat Abu Bakr to resolve the issue? Hazrat Abu Bakr then paid the asking price to free his brother in faith, Hazrat Bilal, which his owner, Umayyah Ibn Khalaf, agreed to. The mother of Hazrat Bilal, Hazrat Hamamah, was also a slave and was freed by Hazrat Abu Bakr.

Hazrat Zunairah was a slave girl. When she embraced Islam, her owner beat her to the extent that her eyesight was taken away. Once again, Hazrat Abu Bakr paid the owner what they wanted and freed her.

Sumayyah Bin Khabbab and her husband Hazrat Yasir both embraced Islam and were the slaves owned by the enemy of Islam, Abu Jahl (the father of ignorance). Abu Jahl beat them both to death due to their testification in Islam. Hazrat Sumayyah was the first female to die in the way of Islam. The Prophet, peace be upon him, would also receive harassment from the people of Makkah. People would throw trash at him while he was walking and praying near the Kabah. However, he always remained calm.

Migration to Abyssinnyah

As the physical abuse kept continuing and getting more severe for the Muslims, It was becoming unbearable, and the Muslims of Makkah were not safe. On the advice of the Prophet, peace be upon him, it was recommended to migrate to Abyssinnyah (Ethiopia). The first migration happened when the Prophet, peace be upon him, was 45 years old. So five years after declaring Prophethood, It is believed that the first batch of Muslims that migrated to Abyssinnyah (Ethiopia) was a group of 15. This consisted of 4 women and 11 men.

Ethiopia during this period had a just king by the name of Najashi (Negus). Although he was a Christian king, he didn't refuse the asylum the Muslims were seeking. Not only did he allow Muslims to enter his territory, but he also allowed them to practice Islam freely. Back in Makkah, there still a lot of Muslims remaining, and more were converting to the religion. The more conversions happened, the more people knew about them, and the non-believers took their anger out on the Muslims through further physical suffering. Over time, more Muslims entered Ethiopia.

Imam Jafar's sermon to King Najashi (Negus)

Imam Jafar (brother of Hazrat Ali and son of Hazrat Abu Talib) and other Muslims attended King Najashi's (Negus) court. Also there were leaders of the Quraysh tribe that arrived in Ethiopia to take the migrant Muslims back to Makkah with the king's permission. Imam Jafar explained to the king the current conditions of Muslims in Makkah and how poorly they were being treated. He further went on to explain the principles of Islam and how we only worship one God. Not numerous idols. Imam Jafar told King Najashi that Prophet Muhammad, peace be upon him, was indeed a prophet and that Allah speaks through him. Imam Jafar mentioned the names of some of the prophets, with Prophet Isa (Jesus) being one of them. Amazed was King Najashi at how they knew the name of Prophet Isa (Jesus). King Najashi then asked Imam Jafar what the Prophet Muahammad, peace be upon him, and what Islam said of Jesus. Imam Jafar responded by reciting a few verses of Surah Maryam (Chapter of Mary in the Quran). This caused somewhat of an emotional effect on King Najashi, as he admired the Muslims love for Maryam (Mary); peace be upon her and Jesus (Prophet Isa). King Najashi then informed the Muslims that they may live in Abyssinnyah for as long as they wish and that they will remain safe. The plan of the Quraysh to manipulate King Najashi so he may not provide a safe haven for the Muslims ultimately failed.

Boycott of Banu Hashim

Abu Talib was the leader of the Banu Hashim tribe, which gave protection to the Prophet. Peace be upon him. Leaders of the other tribes decided to boycott the clan of Banu Hashim. The motive of this boycott was so that the Banu Hashim would eventually surrender their protection for the Prophet, peace be upon him. During this boycott, other clans in Arabia were not allowed to marry any women from the Banu Hashim tribe or give any women to a man of the Banu Hashim clan. Thus ensuring that they were socially excluded from society. It's important to note that not all members of the Banu Hashim tribe were Muslims. Yet they still supported the Prophet, peace be upon him, due to their immense love for him

During this boycott, no one was allowed to trade with Banu Hashim, which affected their financial circumstances heavily. With the economy of the tribe decreasing sharply, this led to a lack of food and water. Alongside all of this, the verbal abuse carried on, and the physical abuse kept getting more severe.

After three years, the boycott ended because the goal of diminishing Islam wasn't planned out. Even during this difficult stage, people were still coming to Islam. On the other hand, some of the leaders who implemented this boycott had died. Over time, other leaders of tribes, even though they were not Muslims, had some empathy for the Muslims suffering, thus ending the boycott.

The passing of Hazrat Abu Talib & Sayyida Khadijah

Three years before the Hijrah (migration to Madinah), the paternal uncle (Hazrat Abu Talib) of the Prophet (peace be upon him) and his wife (Khadijah) both passed away. Hazrat Khadijah was 65 years old when she passed away. Some historians say she passed away on November 22, 619 AD. Although there may be differences with the actual date, What is specific, according to earlier Muslim scholars and historians, is the year 619 AD. She was buried in Makkah, in the cemetery of Jannatul-Muallah.

In the same year, the Prophet's beloved uncle, who protected him and took great care of him, passed away. His approximate age was 82. Hazrat Abu Talib was a clan leader. This facilitated protection for the Prophet; peace be upon him. However, now that my uncle has passed away, that protection would be questioned. Abu Jahl (the father of ignorance) took over the role of chief of the Quraysh tribe after the departure of Abu Talib. Abu Jahl was also a relative of the Prophet; peace be upon him. However, he is the enemy of Islam.

Over the course of the next few years, the Muslims migrating to Abyssinnyah. Many prominent figures had embraced Islam, such as Hazrat Hamzah. Who was the Prophet's uncle? He was feared in Makkah due to his strength and skills on the battlefield. Hazrat Umar, who was also a respectable figure in Makkah, became a Muslim and would later become the third caliph of Islam. Even King Najashi accepted Islam as his religion over a short period of time.

The incident of Ta'if

The people of Makkah were putting the Prophet peace be upon them through an extremely difficult time. The boycott of Banu Hashim has just happened. The Prophet, peace be upon him, lost his protection given by his tribe due to the deaths of his uncle Hazrat Abu Talib and his first wife, Hazrat Khadijah, who passed away. The Prophet, peace be upon him, made the journey to Tai'f in hope for a better settlement of the Muslims than Makkah. Tai'f is around 56 miles from Makkah. The land of Taif was much calmer than Makkah. Ta'if was known for its many orchards of apple trees and rivers by its fields. The people of Ta'if were more educated compared to those in Makkah and were home to many experts in health and astrology at that time. For example, Harith bin Kaladah was a renowned doctor who trained in Persia. Umar Bin Umayyah was an expert in astrology who made many observations of the stars and their speed of travel. When the Prophet, peace be upon him, reached Ta'if, he approached the leaders of that area and invited them to Islam. As the people appeared to be more civilised than those in Makkah, The Prophet, peace be upon him, arrived with sheer hope that they would show sympathy towards him and to the Muslims, whom he hoped could arrive here for safe refuge. After meeting the leaders and many other prominent figures in Ta'if, instead of giving him hope, they made a complete mockery of the Prophet, peace be upon him. Not only did they use vulgar language towards him, they stoned him to the extent that his blessed feet were covered in blood from what was dripping from his blessed head. The blood was so severe that his feet and sandals would be stuck together. Hazrat Zaid Bin Haritha, who accompanied the Prophet, peace be upon him, tried to shield the prophet while the people of Ta'if (including children) would be stoning him. Hazrat Zaid also received injuries and was also bleeding from the amount of stoning that took place towards them.

The Prophet, peace be upon him, and his companion, Zaid Bin Harith, left Ta'if and took refuge under an orchard of grapes. Even in this condition, the Prophet, peace be upon him, prayed 2 rakat (2 units) of Nafl (optional) prayer. A normal person like you and me would've sought revenge and cursed the people of Ta'if. However, this was not the custom of the Prophet, peace be upon him. He prayed to Allah that he was weak and that he could not fulfil the mission he was sent on. He thought Allah was angry with him, and that's maybe why the people of Ta'if abused him. Look how lovely this is, and what an excellent example of the Prophet's humility. Of course, Allah will not be angry at his beloved Prophet. But this is how he felt, and he prayed that Allah would give him strength.

The orchard of grapes that the Prophet, peace be upon him, sought as a haven happened to belong to the chief of Makkah at the time, who was Rabiah. He was on the opposing side of Islam. The sons of Rabia and other chiefs of Makkah were present at exactly the same time. Although they were the enemies of Islam, and the Prophet, peace be upon him, Seeing the severe blood that was dripping from him, they felt sympathy for him.

They rushed one of their salves, Addas, to bring the Prophet, peace be upon him, some grapes. Addas fulfilled this command and watched the Prophet, peace be upon him, closely. When the Prophet, peace be upon him, ate the grapes, he started with the name of God (Bismillah). This is a sunnah that all Muslims should say when beginning to eat or drink. This somewhat amazed Addas, as it was not a custom to start with the name of God when eating or drinking. The Prophet, peace be upon him, then engaged in a conversation with Addas, asking which country he was from and what his religious beliefs were. To which Addas responded that he is a Christian and is from Nineveh (Iraq). The Prophet, peace be upon him, then carried on to say that Nineveh is the city of Prophet Yunus (Jonah). Addas further prompted the Messenger, peace be upon him, to ask how he knew of Prophet Yunus (Jonah). To which the Prophet peace be upon him responded, saying that Prophet Yunus (Jonah) is his brother (brother in faith) and that he was a Prophet and so is he. After hearing this, Addas stood up and kissed the Prophet, peace be upon him, on his head, then his hands, and then his blessed feet. The owners of Addas witnessed this and cursed him as to why he showed a high level of respect and admiration towards the Prophet, peace be upon him. Addas then told his owners that there is nothing better on this earth than the Prophet, peace be upon him, and that he told him something that only a Prophet will be able to tell.

The Prophet, peace be upon him, on his journey back from Ta'if, reached a small mount. When he saw Hazrat Jibraeel (angel Gabriel) approach him, Angel Jibraeel (Gabriel) informed the Prophet, peace be upon him, that the supplication (dua) he made when seeking refuge under the orchard of grapes was heard by Allah. Angel Jibraeel (Gabriel) further informed him that Allah has sent him and will listen to the command that the Prophet peace be upon him orders him to do. Angel Jibraeel (Gabriel) said that he would crush the lands of Ta'if with the two mountains on either side of the area due to the harsh treatment he received from the people of Ta'if. The Prophet, peace be upon him, refused this. He responded to Hazrat Jibraeel (Gabriel) by saying that he hopes their future descendants will embrace Islam. Thus, I left the matter like that.

The Jinns encounter with the Prophet (peace be upon him)

When the Prophet peace be upon him and Hazrat Zaid Bin Haritha were returning from Ta'if, They passed by a place called Nakhlah to offer the Fajr prayers (morning prayers). A group of Jinns were passing by the place and heard the Prophet, peace be upon him, recite the Quran. They stopped for a while, observed the Prophet, peace be upon him, and continued to hear the recitation. They felt a sense of joy while listening to the words of Allah through the best person to have ever stepped foot on this earth. After hearing the recitation, a large group of Jinns accepted Islam at the hands of the Prophet, peace be upon him. It was at this time that a few verses of Surah Jinn (the chapter of Jinn) were revealed.

The splitting of the moon

A group of pagans approached the Prophet, peace be upon him, and commanded that he show them a miracle if he was a true prophet. The Prophet, peace be upon him, said to them, Would they accept Islam if he showed them a miracle? Which they replied yes to. The Prophet, peace be upon him, indicated with his finger towards the moon and split it in two pieces. Instead of the group of pagans accepting Islam, which they agreed to, The hypocrites accused the Prophet, peace be upon him, of being a magician. They say that he uses magic as a form to split the moon or that he casts a spell over their eyes to see illusions. They denied that this was the power of Allah that was given to the Prophet, peace be upon him.

The night journey & ascension (Al-Isra Wal-Mi'raaj)

When the Prophet, peace be upon him, was 50 years old, One of the most crucial events in Islamic history took place. Known as "Al-Isra Wal-Mi'raaj," also known as "Mi'raaj Un-Nabi" (the ascension of the Prophet, peace be upon him), After facing many hardships with the people of Makkah and dealing with the bereavement of his loved ones, The Messenger of Allah, peace be upon him, was taken to the divine presence of Allah. This happened on the 27th of Rajab (the 7th Islamic month).

The Prophet, peace be upon him, slept the night at his cousins house, Umme Hani. She was the daughter of Hazrat Abu Talib and the sister of Hazrat Ali. Her husband was Hubayrah ibn Wah al-Makhzumi. They had two children together, Aqlha and Ja'dah. After having prayed, Isha went to the house of Umme Hani with her family. The Prophet, peace be upon him, went to sleep and was woken by the angel Jibraeel (Gabriel). He was offered a heavenly animal referred to as a "Buraaq." A Buraaq, according to the description by the Prophet, peace be upon him, was larger than a donkey and smaller than a mule. The Buraaq had the ability to travel at the speed of light.

In a time where no trains, planes, supersonic jets, or rockets existed, The Prophet, peace be upon him, rode the buraaq and reached Jerusalem to pray at Masjid al-Aqsa. The buraaq was tied at a specific location where other prophets used to tie their animals. When the Prophet peace be upon him reached Masjid-Al-Aqsa, all the other Prophets that ever existed (124,000 Prophets) were bought to be present at this time. They all met the Prophet, peace be upon him, and he led them in two rakats of Nafl prayer.

The second phase of this journey was when the Prophet, peace be upon him, travelled through the heavens and met with various rophets. In the first heaven, he met Adam; peace be upon him. On the second heaven, he met Prophet Yahyaa (John) and Prophet Isa (Jesus). Peace be upon them. When the Prophet peace be upon him ascended to the third heaven, he met Prophet Yusuf (Joseph). Peace be upon him. On the fourth heaven, he met Prophet Idris (Enoch). Peace be upon him. When he travelled through the fifth heaven, he met Prophet Haroon (Aaron). Peace be upon him. On the sixth heaven, he saw Prophet Musa (Moses), peace be upon him, and on the seventh and final heaven, he met Prophet Ibrahim (Abraham), peace be upon him.

When the Prophet peace be upon him was mounted on the buraaq and was taken through the heavens whilst being accompanied by angel Gabriel (Jibraeel), peace be upon him. Angel Jibraeel could not further progress to a certain extent. After passing the seventh heaven, angel Jibraeel, peace be upon him, bought the Prophet, peace be upon him, to a tree known as "Sidra-Tul-Muntaha" (the lote tree). No one except the Prophet, peace be upon him, can go further than this point. Not even the angels. Jibraeel, peace be upon him, notified the Prophet, peace be upon him, that if he takes one more step beyond the boundary past the lote tree, then he will burn and turn to ashes. This is due to the aurora and the strength of the divine light.

Now the Messenger of Allah, peace be upon him, was directly in front of Allah in his divine court. This is where Allah promised paradise for those who believe in Allah and the final messenger (it doesn't mean all Muslims will go directly to paradise without any compensation for their sins). There are fortunate individuals who will enter paradise without any compensation. While in the divine court of Allah, the last few verses of

Surah Baqarah (Chapter of the Cattle, Chapter 2) were revealed to him. Allah prescribed 50 daily prayers for the Muslims to pray. However, whilst on the journey back to earth, when the Prophet Muhammad, peace be upon him, saw Hazrat Musa (Prophet Moses), he asked him what he received from Allah. The Prophet, peace be upon him, said that he received 50 daily prayers as a gift from God. Prophet Moses, peace be upon him, alerted Prophet Muhammad, peace be upon him, that 50 daily prayers will be a burden for his nation, as the daily prayers were a burden for the nation of Moses. The Prophet Muhammad, peace be upon him, went back to Allah in his divine court and pleaded for the number of prayers to be reduced. Allah then reduced the prayers by 5. Making it a total of 45 daily prayers. On the way back to earth and when stopping at the sixth heaven, Prophet Musa (Moses) asked the Prophet Muhammad, peace be upon him, about the daily prayers. The Prophet Muhammad, peace be upon him, said they have been reduced by five prayers, and now they have 45 daily prayers. Prophet Musa (Moses) once again told the Prophet Muhammad, peace be upon him, that 45 daily prayers will still be a burden and should be further reduced. Once again, the Prophet Muhammad, peace be upon him, requested in the divine court that Allah reduce the prayers. He again reduced it by 5, making the total amount to 40 daily prayers. This incident happened nine times. Where the Prophet Muhammad, peace be upon him, kept going back and forth to Allah and to Prophet Musa (Moses), peace be upon him. Each time the prayers got reduced by five daily prayers, Prophet Musa (Moses) kept telling the Prophet Muhammad, peace be upon him, that those prayers would be a burden for his nation. After the final time of asking Allah to reduce the prayers, it was eventually brought down to five daily prayers. Prophet Musa (Moses) informed the Prophet Muhammad, peace be upon him, that five daily prayers will still be a burden for his nation to carry. The Prophet Muhammad, peace be upon him, stated that he feels shy to keep going back to Allah for the same request of reducing the prayers. Thus, the nation of Muhammad, peace be upon him, was prescribed to perform five daily prayers, and that was the final verdict. Although the prayers were reduced to five daily prayers, Muslims will receive the reward of praying 50 times a day due to the generosity of Allah.

When the Prophet Muhammad, peace be upon him, was taken back to Makkah, to the house of Umme Hani, from the divine presence by mounting on the Buraaq, The Prophet, peace be upon him, informed Umme Hani of what had happened. She told him not to open up publicly about the matter, as people would mock him.

Although this was a lengthy journey from going to Makkah to Jerusalem, then past the seven heavens, and then back to Makkah, In reality, this journey only took up a small portion of the night. This is due to the speed of travel that the Prophet, peace be upon him, was travelling at on the Buraaq. Buraaq is faster than the speed of light. Not only that, when the Prophet peace be upon him was ascending to the heavens, this is a place where time does not exist, and it certainly doesn't exist in the divine court of Allah.

The journey of Al-Isra-Wal-Mi'raaj (the night journey and ascension) proved to be a difficult test for some Muslims and an event of joy for others. Those Muslims at that period of time who had somewhat weak faith (Imaan) were left astonished and questioned about whether Muhammad, peace be upon him, was really a prophet. They saw this as an impossible journey and were left puzzled as to why someone would say this. Some had thought that the Prophet Muhammad, peace be upon him, must've had some sort of mental issue to make this statement. On the other hand, there were strong-faith Muslims who accepted this without a doubt. This further declared to them that their faith in one Allah and that the Prophet Muhammad, peace be upon him, is the last messenger is indeed true. Although the Prophet, peace be upon him, didn't declare what happened on the night journey just yet, The few people he did tell started to tell others, and that's how the word got out to the masses. Abu Bakr (the 1st caliph of Islam) heard about this incident. Without any hesitation, he fully accepted that it happened without any doubt or asking any question as to how it could be possible.

1st pledge of Aqaba

Aqaba is a place next to Makkah. When the Prophet Muhammad, peace be upon him, was 51 years old, six men from Madinah met with him at Aqaba. The Prophet, peace be upon him, informed them of Islam, and they accepted and took their allegiance to Islam at the hands of the Prophet, peace be upon him. Those six men went back to Madinah and informed the people of their city about the Prophet, peace be upon him, and about the religion of Islam. The following year, a few more men from Madinah came to visit the Prophet, peace be upon him, and also accepted Islam at his hands. One of the purposes of the pledge of Aqaba was to slowly bring reform to the world. The following agreement was made by the people of Madinah, and the Prophet peace be upon him. They agreed that they would only worship one Allah, and they promised not to steal.

The agreement further meant they wouldn't kill their daughters and to be just with people. Not to bring false accusations against those innocent. The last pledge was to obey the Prophet Muhammad. Peace be upon him.

2nd pledge of Aqaba

When the Prophet peace be upon him was 53 years old, another larger group of around 70 people met with the Prophet peace be upon him at Aqaba to request that he come to Madinah. Once again, the Prophet, peace be upon him, explained to them the essence of Islam. They accepted Islam at the hands of the Prophet, peace be upon him, and guaranteed that he would be protected when he arrived in Madinah.

Migration to Madinah (Yathrib)

After many years of Muslim suffering, A lot of the companions started to migrate to Madinah. Which back then was known as Yathrib. As the people of Madinah promised Muslims protection, they sought refuge in Madinah as Makkah was becoming severely unsafe. Muslims would emigrate in small or large groups, depending on the circumstances. When the migration happened, this would often happen in secrecy to avoid further deaths or abuse of Muslims. Many people walked from Makkah to Madinah, which is around 280 miles. They would often set off deep in the night to avoid being seen by the Quraysh. As the perfect leader, the Prophet, peace be upon him. He ensured all the Muslims had left Makkah to ensure their safety. With him being the only one left in Makkah, The only ones to remain in Makkah were Hazrat Ali (the cousin of the Prophet, peace be upon him) and Hazrat Abu Bakr Siddique.

Assassination attempt on the Prophet Muhammad (peace be upon him)

As the Muslims have now left to seek refuge in Madinah, the cunning Quraysh created an assassination attempt on the Prophet, peace be upon him. The so-called mastermind behind the plot of the assassination attempt was the enemy of the Prophet, peace be upon him, Abu Jahl. Their plot was to choose the bravest and strongest man from each of the seven clans in Makkah. The seven individuals will then kill the Prophet, peace be upon him, collectively, ensuring that the risk and blame will be divided, making it difficult to hold one person responsible. As mentioned earlier, there were no official governments in Arabia back then, so technically, there was no law. Whatever happened happened based on agreement amongst the tribes. So there would be no trial or no consequences for the murderers. The plan was to break into the Prophet's house while he was sleeping and kill him off there and then. When the 7 thugs broke into the house of the Prophet peace be upon him that night, they found that he was not there, and his cousin, who is known as the lion of Allah due to his strength and bravery, Hazrat Ali, offered to sleep in the Prophet peace be upon him's bed, risking his own life for the Prophet peace be upon him. Once the bandits saw that Hazrat Ali was lying in the Prophet's bed, peace be upon him, they called off the attack. It is certainly not a coincidence that Hazrat Ali just happened to be sleeping in the bed and in the house of the Prophet, peace be upon him. If anything, like many other encounters, this was a form of revelation to the Prophet, peace be upon him. He knew that the enemies of Islam would plot something horrific at this level; therefore, Allah revealed to the Prophet, peace be upon him, the events that were going to occur. The Prophet, peace be upon him, didn't overhear the plot of the assassination, nor did he have to send a spy. This, if anything, is an insight into the knowledge of the Prophet, peace be upon him, of how he knows what will happen in the future and what is happening at numerous places, even though his physical being may be elsewhere.

Some historians say that Hazrat Ali elected himself to risk his life for the Prophet, peace be upon him. Others say that the Prophet, peace be upon him, specifically chose him. None the less, Hazrat Ali wasn't afraid of this. He had no hesitation about this task. The Prophet, peace be upon him, told him that no harm would come to him, which it didn't.

The leaders of Makkah were alerted that the Prophet, peace be upon him, had left the city. They tried to track him down using those who were experts in his footprint at the time, as they believed he couldn't have gone far. The Prophet, peace be upon him, and Hazrat Abu Bakr sought safety in the cave of Thur (Ghar-E-Thur), just on the outskirts of Makkah. The leaders of the Quraysh approached the cave and saw an unbroken spider web and a bird that had built a nest right by the entrance of the cave. As the leaders of Quraysh approached, they discussed amongst themselves that there was no chance that the Prophet peace be upon him could be hiding in there due to the unbroken spider web and bird nest. As forming a spider web and birds building a nest is a lengthy process, On seeing this, the leaders of Quraysh left and searched elsewhere, little knowing that indeed the Prophet, peace be upon him, and Hazrat Abu Bakr were hiding in that cave. Prior to the Prophet peace be upon him and Hazrat Abu Bakr entering the cave, Abu Bakr swept the insides of the cave to make it clean for the Prophet peace be upon him to rest in. He tried to fill as many entrances as possible within the cave of Thur. While in the cave, a snake had bitten Hazrat Abu Bakr. He didn't flinch or make any noise to indicate he was in pain as the Quraysh were close by. He kept glancing at the radiant face of the Prophet, peace be upon him, and was soaking in his spiritual light. The Prophet, peace be upon him, spread some of his blessed saliva over the wound on Hazrat Abu Bakr, which then healed immediately. This is one of many incidents that proves that the Prophet, peace be upon him, was not an ordinary human like you and me. His entire being is a means of blessing for mankind and the universe.

The Prophet, peace be upon him, and Hazrat Abu Bakr stayed in the cave for three days. It is not like today; you can grab a getaway car, head off to the nearest airport or marina, and go to another country in a matter of hours. Most travel was done by foot or with animals such as a camel, horse, mule etc. Not only that, but the blazing heat of Arabia is enough to make the average person faint. In the modern era, skyscrapers and other buildings can cause shade, leading to a somewhat reduced temperature. Back then, it was all desert, making the heat even more unbearable. In order to make sure they were fully safe and that the Quraysh had exhausted their search, they decided to stay in the cave for three days before they could continue with their migration to Madinah (Yathrib). While in the cave, the eldest daughter of Hazrat Abu Bakr Siddique Hazrat Asma would bring them, while his son would keep him updated with any news circulating around Makkah. The family and slaves owned by Hazrat Abu Bakr Siddique remained loyal at all times. They didn't fall into the traps of their egos by accepting the large rewards that were offered to them by the leaders of Makkah to give information on their whereabouts. Some were even offered amounts such as 100 large camels as a reward to give the leaders of Makkah information leading to the capture of the Prophet, peace be upon him.

Entering Madinah

The son of Hazrat Abu Bakr Siddique, Hazrat Abdullah, bought the camels at the cave of Thur so that the Prophet peace be upon him and Hazrat Abu Bakr could mount them for the journey to Madinah. The camel rode by the Prophet, peace be upon him, was called Qaswa. Hazrat Abu Bakr Siddique had purchased two camels to migrate to Madinah. One for himself and one for the Prophet; peace be upon him. Hazrat Abu Bakr Siddique wanted to gift one of the camels (Qaswa) to the Prophet, peace be upon him, but he refused. The Prophet didn't want to accept Qaswa as a gift, as this could be deemed to be taking advantage of a friend, which is not the Prophetic way. Hazrat Abu Bakr paid around 800 dirhams for both the camels. The Prophet, peace be upon him, then paid 400 dirhams for his own camel, called Qaswa. After the purchase was complete, they both set out for Madinah. As the people of Madinah were on the lookout for the Prophet, peace be upon him, and waiting for his arrival, From a far distance, they could see his camel, Qaswa, riding the Prophet, peace be upon him, and entering Madinah.

When the Prophet, peace be upon him, entered Madinah, the people of the city embraced him with love. They were excited to see that the Prophet, peace be upon him, had reached Madinah safely. For many people, this was the first time seeing the Prophet, peace be upon him, and Muslims who migrated there earlier had spoken so highly of him. Furthermore, with the pledges of Aqaba and those that accepted Islam at the hands of the Prophet, peace be upon him, he went back to Madinah and informed the people of the city of how much of an honest and righteous person he was. Therefore, the people of Madinah, who had only heard about the Prophet, peace be upon him, were ecstatic to finally see him and were filled with anticipation. Little girls were singing in praise of the Prophet, peace be upon him, and people were playing drums due to their excitement and offering him a warm welcome into their city after many years of hardship.

The people of Madinah wanted the Prophet, peace be upon him, to stay at their house. But obviously, this offer could not be accommodated as he can only stay in one place. To avoid upsetting anyone and/or hurting their feelings. The people at the time of arrival came to an agreement that they would set the she-camel Qaswa free, and wherever she would sit down, they would build the Prophet's house there. After setting her free, she made her way to a spot close by where the companions greeted the Prophet, peace be upon him. Today, the exact same place is the front entrance of Masjid-e-Nabawi. After Qaswa stopped here, the Prophet, peace be upon him, declared that the Masjid (mosque) would be built here.

Qaswa is no ordinary camel. The Prophet, peace be upon him, his family, and the companions admired Qaswa a lot due to its attachment to the Prophet, peace be upon him. The Prophet, peace be upon him, said that Qaswa is under the command of Allah.

Many events in Islamic history during the era of the Prophet, peace be upon him, could be learned as a result of Qaswa the camel. We can derive Islamic laws (Fiqh), creeds (Aqidah), and theology. During the first Umrah performed by the Prophet, peace be upon him, he made Tawaf of the Kabah while mounted on his camel Qaswa. From this event, it is evident that one may perform Tawaf in the form of a vehicle or, in more serious and genuine cases, a mobility scooter, etc. Even during the Tawaf of Hajj, the Prophet, peace be upon him, used Qaswa. Sections of the Quran were revealed to the Prophet, peace be upon him, while riding on Qaswa. During these moments, Qaswa would crouch down from the standing position as the revelation was heavy and unbearable. During the conquering of Makkah (which will be discussed later), towards the end of the Prophet's time on earth, he entered Makkah whilst riding on Qaswa.

One night, a group of thieves stole Qaswa from its stable alongside other animals and livestock. They also took a female companion of the Prophet, peace be upon him, with them too. The lady managed to free herself and decided to take an animal so she could ride on it so that she could go back to Madinah. Qaswa was the only animal to respond positively to her actions, as she just wanted to escape as quickly as possible. On her way back to Madinah, she felt so relieved that she had escaped and made a vow to God, saying that as a thanksgiving offering, she would slaughter the camel Qaswa and distribute its meat for a feast. On her return, she informed the locals of what had happened. The companions of the Prophet, peace be upon him, went in search to find out who the bandits were and to recover the stock and return it to its rightful owners. This female approached the Prophet, peace be upon him, requesting if she could have the camel back as she had taken an oath to slaughter Qaswa as a thanksgiving offering. The Prophet, peace be upon him, informed her that she cannot fulfil a vow on something she doesn't own. This is an Islamic legal ruling for the whole Muslim nation. You cannot or shouldn't promise anything that you cannot fulfil for something that is not in your possession. She was then required to pay for the compensation for her vow (the monetary equivalent of the camel).

From Qaswa, we can learn how to love the Prophet, peace be upon him, as it shares many historical events. Even after the Prophet, peace be upon him, left this world, Qaswa couldn't bear the loss. She stopped eating and drinking and cried to the extent that she became blind. Qaswa passed away 2-4 weeks after the passing of the Prophet. Peace be upon him.

From these stories, we can learn Islamic law on how to treat animals with love.

After entering Madinah, while the Masjid (Mosque) and the house of the Prophet, peace be upon him, were being built, he resided in the house of Hazrat Ayyub Al-Ansari.

The beginning of the call to prayer (Azaan)

Since the declaration of Prophethood (when the Prophet peace be upon him was 40), there was no call to prayer (Azaan). It was only after the migration to Madinah that the Muslim population grew. Therefore, something needed to be done to announce the times of prayer. The companions had a discussion, and various points were raised. Actions such as raising a flag, blowing on a whistle like the Jews, and ringing a bell like the Christians were considered but disapproved by the Prophet, peace be upon him. Some companions even suggested lighting a fire from a high, raised place, but the Prophet, peace be upon him, declined. These resembled other religions, which was one of the reasons why these methods did not get approved. Numerous companions saw a dream in the coming days. That the call to prayer should be recited with the words of God and the Prophet, peace be upon him. Two of the companions to see a dream were Hazrat Abdullah Bin Zaid and Hazrat Umar Faruq. They saw someone teaching them the words of the Azaan (call of prayer). In the morning, they both approached the Prophet, peace be upon him, and informed him of the dream. The Prophet, peace be upon him, replied that he also saw a dream of the words of the Azaan being revealed to him. The companions, at the request of the Prophet, peace be upon him, then taught the words of the Azaan (call of prayer) to Hazrat Bilal. Hazrat Bilal was the main person responsible for calling the prayer during the time of the Prophet, peace be upon him, as he was chosen specially for this due to his melodious voice.

Islamic unity

As the number of Muslims increased, A sense of unity had to be established. The people of Arabia came from a background where wealth and authority gave someone rights, and if you were a slave or were poor, you had no rights. Furthermore, racism was an issue back then as it is today, and people of many tribes had grudges against each other due to historical political issues. If the Muslims wanted good, then this had to come to an end. The Prophet, peace be upon him, created a treaty among all people who were Muslims, regardless of their socio-economic background and skin colour. This caused the Muslims to unite, put their differences aside, and learn to love and respect one another.

Battle of Badr

The battle of Badr is the first fight in Islamic history to take place between truth and falsehood. The Muslims were outnumbered, having an army of 313 men compared to 1,000 of the opposition. The non-Muslims (Quraysh) were far more well equipped than the Muslims, with more horses, camels, and armour. The Quraysh approximately had 700 camels and around 100 horses to mount during the battle. Whereas the Muslims only had one horse (some sources state two horses) between an army of 313.

It can be said that the people of Arabia would see how serious the religion of Islam was becoming. People were not afraid to fight for their beliefs. The main purpose of this battle was to capture the caravan of Abu Sufyan, which contained a lot of possessions that belonged to the Muslims, before leaving Makkah for Madinah. As the Muslims had to leave Makkah, the possessions that remained were being sold for large profits, and as any rightful owner would, they wanted their assets back.

The day before Badr, the Quraysh arrived earlier than the Muslims at the field where the battle would take place. As they got their first, they occupied the wells, ensuring they had water available for their use.

Islam wasn't just a cult, as some may have thought. The battle of Badr, as well as the battles to come in Islamic history, would see fathers killing their own sons and vice versa. Standing up to their beliefs and showing how passionate they were for the cause of Islam. The battle of Badr took place on the 17th of Ramadan (some historians say the 12th of Ramadan). Some of the most prominent enemies of Islam would be killed during the battle. The victory of the Muslims ensured that they had become a strong force across Arabia and were not a group to take lightly, as others had thought. During the battle of Badr, as the Muslims were outnumbered, the Prophet, peace be upon him, prayed to Allah to grant them victory. The prayer of the Prophet, peace be upon him, was answered, and Allah sent angels to take part in this battle to aid the Muslims.

The battle ended with the Muslims having 14 casualties and the Quraysh losing 70 of their men. Including Abu Jahl. The Muslims held some of the Quraysh captive as prisoners. They were treated with respect and were not humiliated. Although the Prophet, peace be upon him, was a mercy to mankind and showered those around him with love and care, This treatment, for some, could be ironic to grasp. However, it is important to know that this had to happen for the Quraysh to take the Muslims seriously for the faith to dominate and grow to what it did towards the end of the Prophet's time on this earth. Some companions requested that the captives of Quraysh should be killed, but this was rejected by the Prophet, peace be upon him. It was the final decision of the Prophet, peace be upon him, to hold them captive and give them opportunities to redeem themselves. The prisoners could've accepted Islam, which would have qualified them to be free. Another proposition was that those held captive could teach Muslims how to read and write for those who weren't strongly equipped with education. There was an alternative. If anyone wished to free the prisoners, they would be charged a heavy sum of money for their release. The money would then be used to support Muslims with their needs. For example, construction of houses, mosques, or to fund further battles (equipping the army). Unlike other empires around the world during and/or before the time of the Prophet, peace be upon. Prisoners would be treated with respect and were well fed. Compared to other dynasties and governments around the globe, where prisoners would be starved and tortured, After the battle had finished, The economic situation and the power of Muslims increased.

Battle of Uhud

The Quraysh, suffering a loss and causalities at Badr, wanted to take their revenge on the Muslims at the battle of Uhud. Uhud is a mountain in Madinah where many tourists still visit today to see the site where the battle took place. The Quraysh prepared a much larger army compared to what they did at Uhud. The Quraysh had an army of around 3,000 men. Including 3,000 camels and 200 horsemen. The Muslims were once again outnumbered. Their army consisted of 700 men, 50 archers, and 4 horsemen. The Muslim army, under the command of the Prophet, peace be upon him, ensured a strategy of placing the archers on the mountain while the actual battle was taking place. The Muslims could be assured that a defence strategy was implemented to avoid them being attacked from the back. The order was given that the archers do not leave their place, no matter what the circumstances are.

The Muslim army set out early in the morning towards Uhud. They arrived at the mountain and performed the Fajr (morning) prayers. Knowing that the Quraysh (Makkan) army was three times the size. The Prophet, peace be upon him, delivered a sermon to the Muslims to encourage them. Once the battle had begun, the Muslims had the upper hand, fighting with fierce strength. However, it was not long until some of the Muslims, in particular the archers, were getting quite overwhelmed with excitement as they could see their fellows dominate the battleground. Even though the senior army commanders and the Prophet, peace be upon him, ordered them to remain at their stations, They disobeyed this order and started to celebrate the victory of the battle far too soon. Even though the battle was still going on, This caused the archers to move from the stations and for the Quraysh to attack them from various angles. It caused many Muslims to die at Uhud, which led to the loss of the battle. The main goal for the Quraysh in this battle was once again to have the Prophet, peace be upon him, killed so they could destroy Islam. However, this failed.

Hazrat Hamzah, the uncle of the Prophet, was a feared person in Makkah during the early stages of Islam. His conversion to the religion was a shocking moment for the people of Makkah, as they didn't think someone of his calibre would defend a new religion. He was known for his courageous strength. Knowing this, the Quraysh wanted to take him out. They specifically chose someone to participate amongst their army who was greatly skilled in using a spear. They knew that if they got close to Hazrat Hamzah, he would have an advantage due to his skills with the sword and his strength. During the battle of Uhud, the most prominent loss to the Muslims was Hazrat Hamzah, who was killed by the individual specifically hired to kill him by the spear, which is what happened.

During the battle, the Prophet peace be upon him was attacked by Utbah Bin Abi Waqas, who threw stones at the Prophet peace be upon him, causing him to lose a few of his teeth. For safety, the Prophet, peace be upon him, and some of the companions climbed up the mountain of Uhud to have a better view of the battlefield. The Muslim army consisted of some female warriors too, who were stronger and more courageous than some men. One of them was Nusaybah Bin Kab. During the battle of Uhud, she guarded the Prophet, peace be upon her, on numerous occasions. On the battlefield, when the Quraysh were searching for the Prophet, peace be upon him, she would battle them with her sword, and from the mountains she would shoot arrows at the enemy. Not only was she strong, but it was difficult to match her speed. She would go around the battlefield in extremely short periods of time. Sometimes you may watch these modern Hollywood films and wonder where they get their ideas from. If there was a real-life superwoman, then it certainly would've been Nusaybah. Her husband and two sons also participated in this war. There were many other women who supported the Muslims during the days of battle in numerous ways. Some would carry the water jugs or buckets, and some helped with aiding those injured with their wounds. Considering Islam has this negative representation in the media for always suppressing women and so forth, it is bizarre, as women were the backbone of Islamic history.

It is important to understand that Islam has laws for every matter. Even during warfare. No civilian, woman, or child can be harmed by Muslims during a battle. Even to cut a tree unjustly is not allowed. What occurred after the battle of Uhud was more disturbing than the battle itself. The wife of Abu Sufyan, who was Hind, amputated the body parts of the dead Muslims at Uhud. Even though Hazrat Hamzah was killed, after the battle, she ordered for him to be cut open and to have his heart and liver taken out. She took a bite of his liver but could not swallow it. Some women amputated the ears and noses of the Muslim soldiers and turned them into a garland-like necklace to wear when they returned from Uhud back to Makkah to show off what they had done to the Muslims.

Battle of Khandaaq (battle of the trench)

The battle of Khandaaq (the battle of the trench) has a somewhat different context compared to previous battles. Prior to this, it was the Quraysh fighting the Muslims. However, now the enemies of Islam are combined with various other tribes across the Arabian Peninsula. Other pagan tribes across Arabia and the Jewish tribes performed an alliance with the Quraysh in hope of killing off Islam, and the Prophet peace be upon him. The commander of this conglomerate was Abu Sufian, who led previous armies against Islam. He wrote a letter to the Prophet, peace be upon him, notifying him that he would bring the strongest army against the Muslims and that they should refrain from fighting back. The Prophet, peace be upon him, replied that they would not succeed and that victory would be with the Muslims. The Prophet, peace be upon him, held a meeting with his companions to come up with a strategy to defeat the enemies of Islam. Hazrat Salmaan Farsi came up with the idea of digging a trench around Madinah to avoid any invasion. The Prophet, peace be upon him, agreed to this, and the Muslims united to dig a trench around the city of Madinah. It was during the winter when the Muslims were digging the trenches. Their morale was low due to the cold, tiredness, and hunger of the Muslims, but it didn't stop them from carrying out their task due to the love of the Prophet, peace be upon him, and the unity of their fellow Muslims. To boost morale, many of the companions and the Prophet, peace be upon him himself, would recite poetry aloud whilst digging the trenches. The trench was approximately 9 metres wide, 5–6 kilometres long, and around 4-5 kilometres deep.

After three days of intense digging, the companions became severely hungry, with not even a piece of bread at their disposal. Hazrat Jabir sought permission from the Prophet, peace be upon him, to go to his house and see if there was any food available. Hazrat Jabir's wife said to him that there was barely enough to make bread and a small goat that they could slaughter. He knew this would not be enough to feed all the companions. As the wife of Hazrat Jabir was preparing the food, he went and told the Prophet, peace be upon him, that food was of little quantity and he should come to their house with a few companions only. The Prophet, peace be upon him, responded to what was prepared. Hazrat Jabir replies with some meat from a small goat and bread. The Prophet, peace be upon him, said that is a lot of food and not to worry about their being any shortfalls. The Prophet, peace be upon him, entered the house and blessed the flour of barley and the cooking pot containing the meat. He further stated to Hazrat Jabir that his wife should continue to prepare the food. Amazed was Hazrat Jabir that, due to the blessing of the Prophet, peace be upon him, around 1,000 companions ate as much as they could with that small goat and the minor quantity of flour they had. Even after feeding people in large quantities, food still remained.

The Muslims had to ensure the trench was quickly dug to avoid any unexpected attack from the opposition. The trenches were completed in six days. The women and children of Madinah were put into towers within the city. The popular valleys of Madinah had been enclosed with tall walls, making the entire Madinah look like a fort. The opposition arrived and camped close by with their army of 10,000, consisting of battalions of combined tribes. The Muslims, with their army of 3,000, camped behind the trench. The battle took place over 30 days. Each day, the enemies of Islam faced losses and could not cross the trench. Their animals ended up wounded, and the strong winds of Madinah made it difficult for them to cross the trench. This ended with the Muslims winning the battle by fighting from the trenches.

Between the battle of Uhud and the battle of the trench, the Prophet, peace be upon him, married numerous times. Even after the battle of the trenches, numerous other battles took place. However, to keep the book slightly short and not bore the readers of the book, I have decided not to include them. Towards the end of this chapter, a further reading list will be provided for those who wish to dwell on detailed incidents from various other stories during the life of the Prophet, peace be upon him.

Laws imposed in the 6th Hijrah (6 years after the migration to Madinah)

Some of the outlines of Islamic laws imposed in the 6th Hijrah are given below.

Hajj was made mandatory for Muslims for those able to if they had the necessity of wealth and health. One should not perform Hajj if they owe someone money, as the debt should be paid first. As Hajj requires a lot of physical strength, one should perform Hajj when they are physically fit so they do not burden anyone else.

The prayer for rain also started this year. There had not been rainfall for a while, which caused the wells and plants to dry. Cattle and people were dying of hunger due to a lack of crops. The companions requested that the Prophet, peace be upon him, pray for rain. The Prophet, peace be upon him, led the companions in two units (Rakat) of prayer with loud recitation. In the first unit (Rakat), he recited Surah Al-Fatiha (the second chapter of the Quran), then Surah Al-Ala (the 87th chapter of the Quran). In the second unit (Rakat), he recited Surah Al-Fatiha and Surah Al-Ghashiya (the 88th chapter of the Quran). After the prayer, the Prophet, peace be upon him, prayed to Allah to bestow rain. As the congregation still remained seated, The clouds turned dark, and the rain was continuous for 7 days and 7 nights.

The prohibition of alcohol came into effect this year.

وَمِن ثَمَرَٰتِ ٱلنَّخِيلِ وَٱلْأَعْنَٰبِ تَتَّخِذُونَ مِنْهُ سَكَرًا وَرِزْقًا حَسَنًا إِنَّ فِى ذَٰلِكَ لَآيَةً لِّقَوْمٍ يَعْقِلُونَ

Translation: And from the fruits of palm trees and grapevines you derive intoxicants1 as well as wholesome provision. Surely in this is a sign for those who understand. (Surah al-Nahl, Verse 67)

يَسْـَٔلُونَكَ عَنِ ٱلْخَمْرِ وَٱلْمَيْسِرِ قُلْ فِيهِمَآ إِثْمٌ كَبِيرٌ وَمَنَـٰفِعُ لِلنَّاسِ وَاثْمُهُمَآ أَكْبَرُ مِن نَّفْعِهِمَا وَيَسْـَٔلُونَكَ مَاذَا يُنفِقُونَ قُلِ ٱلْعَفْوَ كَذَٰلِكَ يُبَيِّنُ ٱللَّهُ لَكُمُ ٱلْءَايَـٰتِ لَعَلَّكُمْ تَتَفَكَّرُونَ

Translation: "They ask you ˹O Prophet˺ about intoxicants and gambling. Say, "There is great evil in both, as well as some benefit for people—but the evil outweighs the benefit." They also ask you ˹O Prophet˺ what they should donate. Say, "Whatever you can spare." This is how Allah makes his revelations clear to you believers, so perhaps you may reflect." (Surah Baqarah verse 219)

Some companions would hold feasts and provide alcohol as the beverage. One of the companions led prayers whilst slightly intoxicated and kept making major errors in the recitation of the prayer, thus changing its meaning. This is when the 43rd verse of Surah An-Nisa was revealed:

يَـٰٓأَيُّهَا الَّذِينَ اٰمَنُوا لَا تَقْرَبُوا الصَّلَوٰةَ وَأَنْتُمْ سُكْرى حَتّٰى تَعْلَمُوا مَا تَقُولُونَ وَلَا جُنُبًا إِلَّا عَابِرِى سَبِيلٍ حَتّٰى تَغْتَسِلُوا وَإِنْ كُنْتُمْ مَّرْضٰى أَوْ عَلٰى سَفَرٍ أَوْ جَآءَ أَحَدٌ مِّنْكُمْ مِّنَ الْغَآئِطِ أَوْ لٰمَسْتُمُ النِّسَآءَ فَلَمْ تَجِدُوا مَآءً فَتَيَمَّمُوا صَعِيدًا طَيِّبًا فَامْسَحُوا بِوُجُوهِكُمْ وَاَيْدِيكُمْ إِنَّ اللّٰهَ كَانَ عَفُوًّا غَفُورًا

Translation: "O People who Believe! Do not approach the prayer when you are intoxicated until you have the sense to understand what you say, nor in the state of impurity until you have bathed except while traveling; and if you are ill or on a journey or one of you returns from answering the call of nature or you have cohabited with women, and you do not find water, then cleanse (yourself) with clean soil - therefore stroke your faces and your hands with it; indeed, Allah is Most Pardoning, and Forgiving."

يَٰٓأَيُّهَا ٱلَّذِينَ ءَامَنُوٓاْ إِنَّمَا ٱلْخَمْرُ وَٱلْمَيْسِرُ وَٱلْأَنصَابُ
وَٱلْأَزْلَٰمُ رِجْسٌ مِّنْ عَمَلِ ٱلشَّيْطَٰنِ فَٱجْتَنِبُوهُ لَعَلَّكُمْ
تُفْلِحُونَ ٩٠ إِنَّمَا يُرِيدُ ٱلشَّيْطَٰنُ أَن يُوقِعَ بَيْنَكُمُ
ٱلْعَدَٰوَةَ وَٱلْبَغْضَآءَ فِى ٱلْخَمْرِ وَٱلْمَيْسِرِ وَيَصُدَّكُمْ عَن
ذِكْرِ ٱللَّهِ وَعَنِ ٱلصَّلَوٰةِ فَهَلْ أَنتُم مُّنتَهُونَ

Translation: "O believers! Intoxicants, gambling, idols, and drawing lots for decisions1 are all evil of Satan's handiwork. So shun them so you may be successful. Satan's plan is to stir up hostility and hatred between you with intoxicants and gambling and to prevent you from remembering Allah and praying. Will you not then abstain?" (Surah al-Maaidah, Verse 90-91)

When this verse was revealed, the Muslims threw away the remaining alcohol they had at their disposal into the drains of Madinah. It was to the extent that the streets of Madinah looked like heavy rain had fallen on the city. That's how much alcohol was consumed prior to prohibition.

Muslims marrying polytheists were forbidden for both men and women.

7th year of Hijrah

This year is known as the golden age of Islam. The Prophet, peace be upon him, sent letters to various monarchs and leaders across the world inviting them to Islam. He wrote letters to the king of Abyssinnyah, who was Negus (Najashi), Caesar of Rome, and the king of Iran, who was Parvez Bin Hurmuz at the time. A letter was sent to King Maqoqus of Egypt. Harith Bin Abi Shiman was sent the same letter as the chief of Arab Christians.

King Najashi (Negus) of Abussinnyah showed the upmost respect when receiving the letter. He even got up from his throne, sat on the floor, and read the letter out to those present. This is when King Najashi accepted Islam as his faith and wrote a letter back to the Prophet, peace be upon him, informing him of his acceptance. When the letter reached Heraclius, Caesar of Rome, he wanted to get a better understanding of who the Prophet, peace be upon him, was. Abu Sufyan, who led armies against the Prophet, peace be upon him, but was also his first cousin, was in Gaza at the time for business, as were some of the people of Rome. Caesar informed his men in Gaza to bring him an Arab so he could question them about the Prophet, peace be upon him. They bought Abu Sufyan in the presence of Heraclius. The Caesar of Rome asked him who was his closest relative. Abu Sufyan said that it was him and that they were first cousins. Heraclius asked Abu Sufyan numerous questions about the lineage of the Prophet, peace be upon them, and their financial wellbeing. Abu Sufyan told the truth even though, at the time, he was an enemy of Islam. He didn't want to be known as a great liar, so he gave in and told the truth about the Prophet, peace be upon him, and how he was a just man. The companion responsible for delivering the letter to Caesar was Dhiya Al-Kalbi. After reading the letter and asking Abu Sufyan, Caesar took Dhiya Al-Kalbi to his private seclusion room and informed him that previous holy scriptures had informed him that the final prophet, by the name of Muhammad, would appear and knew of his qualities. He accepted Islam as his faith, but knew the people of Rome and the Christians would turn against him. Caesar went to the church and told the congregation that they should accept Islam and the final prophet as he did. This enraged the Christians to the extent that they launched an attack on Caeser there and then. Heraclius died of injuries, and Dhiya Al-Kalbi managed to escape the attack.

Not all leaders and monarchs accepted Islam in the letter that was sent by the Prophet, peace be upon him. As leaders and kings, they thought that they were the chosen ones; they had arrogance about why they should submit to a prophet who was poor when they themselves were kings.

The king of Iran tore the letter and declined the invitation to Islam. Parvez, the king of Iran, wrote a letter to the governor of Yemen, who was Bazaan at the time. They requested for the Prophet, peace be upon him, to be arrested and for him to surrender. Upon hearing this news, the Quraysh rejoiced and thought this would be the end of the road for the Prophet. Peace be upon him and Islam. Bazaan sent a deputy of his, named Bariowia, and an Iranian named Khar Khusrah to Madinah with the letter for it to reach the Prophet peace be upon him and for him to bring the Prophet peace be upon him to the court of the king of Iran. The Prophet, peace be upon them, knew that they would arrive and facilitated comfortable accommodation for them. When they arrived in front of the Prophet, peace be upon him, they handed the letter to him and requested that he go back with Bariowia to see the king of Iran. The Prophet, peace be upon him, told them to rest and that the meeting would continue the following day. That night, the angel Jibraeel (Gabriel) appeared before the Prophet, peace be upon him, to inform him that the king of Iran (Parvez) was murdered by his own son Sheroia after stabbing him in the stomach. The following morning, the Prophet, peace be upon him, told Bariowia and Khar Khusrah that they should go to their master and say that the lord of Muhammad killed their lord last night on the 7th hour of the night. He further described how Sheroia climbed on his father's chest, stabbing him in the stomach. Bariowia and Khar did not believe this and were angered by this statement, not knowing that it was indeed true. Once returning to their land, they found out the news was certainly correct. Bazaan believed in the final prophet and declared his faith in Islam. Many others in Iran accepted the message of Islam, and they sent the news to the Prophet, peace be upon him, of their acceptance.

Battle of Khaybar

Khaybar is north of Madinah. Approximately 106 miles apart. During the time of the Prophet, peace be upon him, Khaybar consisted of mainly Jewish tribes. Khaybar had a vast amount of resources when it came to fruit orchards and grain fields. After the Muslims first arrived in Madinah on their migration, The main Jewish tribes broke their treaty and were forced to leave Madinah. The Jewish tribes settled in Khaybar. The main tribes consisted of:

1. Banu Nadir

2. Banu Qaynuqa

3. Banu Qurayzah

Since they were forced to leave their homes in Madinah, They had strong hatred for Muslims and had always wanted to seek revenge. When the Prophet, peace be upon him, arrived in Madinah for the migration, he concluded a treaty that would allow people of all faiths and colours to live in peace. People would be free to practice their faith and obligations without any disturbance from those of other faiths. Places of worship for all religions will be secured, and no one should cheat one another or break the trust between the parties. Another important factor in the treaty was that no one would be allowed to oppress anyone. With this treaty, it caused more people to accept Islam as their faith and recognise that indeed, Muhammad, peace be upon him, was the messenger of Allah.

Seeing this, the Jews grew more resentful of Muslims. The Jews were still struggling to digest the victory of Muslims in previous battles and wanted to take matters into their own hands. While the Prophet, peace be upon him, was in the marketplace, addressing people about Islam and believing in one God, The Jews threatened the Muslims. Which was a breach of peace in the treaty. To escalate the matter. A Muslim woman visited a jeweller in Qaynuqa, where she was harassed to uncover her face. The jeweller, who was a Jew, pinned her clothes down, so as she got up, her body became revealed. A Muslim man witnessed this and then killed the jeweller. The Jews then attacked that Muslim man, which killed him. This is what led to the Battle of Khaybar, as the Jews broke the treaty. Regardless of these incidents, the Jews were already planning an attack on Madinah.

Historians and early Muslim scholars state that the battle of Khaybar occurred in the Islamic month of Muharram (1st Islamic month) on the 7th day. The Muslim army consisted of 1600 soldiers, with 200 of them on horses. The opposition army consisted of 10,000 Jews. The Prophet, peace be upon him, and the Muslim army entered Khaybar during the night. It was not the custom of the Prophet, peace be upon him, nor of the Muslims to wage war in the dark. So they rested until the morning (Fajr) prayer. The Jews knew of the rumour that the Muslims would launch an attack on them, but they didn't think they would actually do it. Due to the large army and resources of the Jews, Khaybar was split into numerous sections. The Prophet, peace be upon him, divided his army into smaller groups to take over various areas of Khaybar. As the battle commenced, it ended with the Muslims losing 15 of their men and the Jews losing 93. Thus leading to a Muslim victory. Now that Khaybar was under Muslim rule, the Jews were still given permission to reside there. However, they were to work in the crop field, with the Muslims taking a profit from their crops as they had the right to exclude them if they wished.

Hazrat Ali, the 4th caliph of Islam and the cousin and son-in-law of the Prophet, peace be upon him, played a crucial role during the battle of Khaybar. He was responsible for holding the flag of Islam during the battle and showed his immense strength during this time.

In the 7th Hijrah (7th year after migration), temporary marriages became forbidden in Islam, as declared by the Prophet, peace be upon him. Unfortunately, the Shia community still practices temporary marriages (Mutah). They believe it to be greater than Hajj and Umrah. In a temporary marriage, there is no need for witnesses, and no rules are applied. This degrading act for women was abolished by the Prophet, peace be upon him, to give women a high status in Islam.

Conquest of Makkah

Prior to the conquest of Makkah. A treaty was agreed upon among the Muslims and the Quraysh. This was a peace treaty known as "the treaty of Hudaybiyah." This was to prevent further battles between the Muslims and their opposition, which was more than the Quraysh, as we learned in the battle of Uhud. The treaty was supposed to last for 10 years and allow all parties to live peacefully. This would further allow the Muslims to perform the minor pilgrimage (Umrah) the following year without any bloodshed. However, the treaty was broken after two years by a confederate tribe of Quraysh known as Banu Bakr, who helped launch an attack on a tribe that allied with the Muslims. Which is known to be Banu Khuza'aah. The treaty was broken in Makkah. Due to the spiritual insight of the Prophet, peace be upon him, he knew the treaty was broken before the news reached Madinah. The Prophet, peace be upon him, started to prepare the army to march into Makkah. The Quraysh were frustrated that their allies (Banu Bakr) broke this treaty and sent Abu Sufyan from Makkah to Madinah to embed the trust of the Muslims. However, he was turned away. The Quraysh knew that the Muslims were a true threat due to their large and growing numbers. By this time, Islam had begun to spread across the world.

The Prophet, peace be upon him, arranged for an army of 10,000 Muslims to take over Makkah. The army of 10,000 was split into four sections. This allowed the Muslims to enter Makkah from four sides. The Muslim army left Madinah on the 10th of Ramadan and reached Makkah on the 17th of Ramadan. The people of Makkah thought that Muslims would take revenge for what the Quraysh did to them at the Battle of Uhud. The people of Makkah thought they would be killed as they saw the large Muslim army enter the city. This was not the case. The Prophet, peace be upon him, was riding on his camel, Qaswa. His nose was touching the back of the camel's neck, in humility to Allah and giving him thanks for the victory of the Muslims. When entering Makkah and on his camel, the Prophet peace be upon him was reciting Surah Al-Fath (the chapter of the victory), the 48th chapter of the Quran. The Prophet, peace be upon him and the Muslims, headed straight towards the Kabah. The Prophet, peace be upon him, went around the Kabah and destroyed the idols surrounding it. The Prophet, peace be upon him, requested the keys to open the doors of the Kabah, which were given to him. He entered the Kabah and destroyed the idols that remained within the house of God. After performing Tawaf (circulation of the Kabah), the Prophet, peace be upon him, requested Hazrat Bilal to go on top of the Kabah to call the Azaan (call to prayer). The companions set up a tent for the Prophet, peace be upon them, in a place called Hujun. This is where his first wife, Khadijah, was buried. The Prophet, peace be upon him, wanted to spend time by her grave, for she heavily supported him without any doubts when most others turned away from him. She didn't live to see Islam spread vastly across the world or the conquest of Makkah. This is a sign of gratitude that the Prophet, peace be upon him, had for his first wife.

After the conquest of Makkah was complete, the people of Makkah saw the true force of Islam and how rapidly they grew in numbers and in strength. Many of the residents of Makkah converted to Islam without force. It was now that the people of Makkah seemed to be the minority. Abu Sufyan, who once was the enemy of the Prophet, peace be upon him, converted to Islam before the conquering of Makkah. His wife, Hind Bint Utbah, converted to Islam after Makkah was taken over by the Muslims. Although she was the one that chewed the heart of Hazrat Hamzah, the uncle of the Prophet, peace be upon him, and ordered her slave to rip open his body after being killed in the battle of Uhud, The Prophet, peace be upon him, still forgave her. She appeared in front of the Prophet, peace be upon him, fully veiled, due to her shame and fear that she would be killed by the Muslims for all the pain and agony she caused them over the years. But no harm came to her or her husband. This is an example of how merciful the Prophet, peace be upon him, was.

The sons of Abu Lahab, who are Utbah and Mautab, converted to Islam. Even though Abu Lahab is promised hell for eternity, as stated in the Quran in Surah Lahab (Chapter of Lahab), it didn't stop his sons from being wise enough to accept Islam. They both later went on to fight in other battles for Islam, which are not mentioned in this book.

The Prophet, peace be upon him, stayed in Makkah for 15 days after conquering it. Within this time, he set up the administration of the city and its laws. He destroyed temples of idol worship. The Prophet, peace be upon him, appointed Muaaz Bin Jabal to teach Islamic practices to the people of Makkah. He further appointed Attab Bn Usaid to be the governor of Makkah, who was only 21 at the time. Unlike now, in the corporate world, people may be discriminated against in higher corporate roles due to their age and experience. The Prophet, peace be upon him, recognised his skills and ambition and saw him fit for the role. The religious ban on fornication and adultery became more strict. This was severely common throughout Arabia, and brothels would have flags outside their homes as an indication of these acts. To prevent new Muslims from falling into this trap and to create a new society of purity and faith, these acts were abolished. Gambling was another drug in society back then, as it is today. This also came to an end during the Conquest of Makkah. The 15 days the Prophet peace be upon him stayed in Makkah were a total cleaning process of society and to root Islamic beliefs amongst the communities.

Hajjatul-Wadaa (farewell Hajj)

The farewell hajj (pilgrimage) is the final hajj the Prophet peace be upon did in his life. Prior to this, he performed Umrah (a minor pilgrimage) and Hajj numerous times. The Prophet, peace be upon him, had a few objectives during this hajj, as he knew this would be his last hajj. The first objective is to show Muslims how hajj should be performed. Secondly, he wanted as many Muslims as possible to be present at this Hajj as he delivered sermons throughout this pilgrimage. Lastly, after all the decades of struggles, battles, and pain he absorbed, this Hajj could be seen as a celebration for all the efforts that he put into establishing Islam, along with those that supported him.

The Prophet, peace be upon him, mounted his she-camel Qaswa and made the journey to Makkah from Madinah with his followers and present wives. Once entering Makkah and performing the rituals of Tawaaf (Circulation of the Kabah), run and walk between the mountains of Safa and Marwah. The Prophet, peace be upon him, walked to Mina, as this is a requirement for those performing Hajj. Having stayed there night there. The Prophet, peace be upon him, and the rest of those performing Hajj made their way to Mount Arafat, where a tent was set up for the Prophet, peace be upon him. After Maghrib prayers in Arafat, the Prophet peace be upon him mounted his camel Qaswa and went to the valley of Batan, where he delivered a sermon teaching the practices of Islam to the followers present. During this sermon, the Prophet, peace be upon him, emphasised the need to treat women with kindness and that spouses have rights over each other. He reminded his nation to hold onto the Quran and his teachings (Sunnah) firmly so they may not go astray while on earth. The Prophet, peace be upon him, stated that Muslims are brothers to one another and that Muslims must not take any possession without consent. He further mentioned that Muslims should not subject themselves to oppression. He mentioned that Usuary is forbidden for Muslims. He stated that those who oppress someone will be oppressed themselves. The concept of destiny was included in this sermon, stating that people cannot achieve more than what Allah has written for them. The Prophet, peace be upon him, taught Muslims that if something is borrowed, it should be returned to its rightful owner. Any loans taken out should be paid back. The Prophet, peace be upon him, ended the sermon by raising his index finger to the sky and saying, "Oh Allah, be witness to them. After addressing the sermon, the Prophet peace be upon him requested Hazrat Bilal to call for the prayer (Azaan) for Zuhur (afternoon prayer), and the Prophet peace be upon him led the Zuhur prayer and the Asr (late afternoon) prayer for that day. He then mounted his camel Qaswa, went back to his tent, and supplicated Allah. During the season of Hajj, it is mandatory for Muslims who are mature in age to offer an animal as a sacrifice. The minimum requirement is to offer a goat. This should be distributed amongst the poor, friends, and neighbors, and one is allowed to take some for themselves if they want, but it is not mandatory. In the last Hajj of the Prophet, peace be upon him, he offered 63 camels to be sacrificed. Each camel represents the 63 years he lived (the Prophet, peace be upon him, was also 63 during his final Hajj). He, peace be upon him, slaughtered 26 camels with his own hands. The remaining were slaughtered by Hazrat Ali on his behalf. Each camel came towards the Prophet peace be upon on their own account, stretching its own neck before him to be slaughtered by him or Hazrat Ali. The Prophet, peace be upon him, also sacrificed a cow on behalf of his wives. As it's a requirement (it is Sunnah for men to shave the entire head), It is mandatory to at least cut 2 inches of the hair for both men and women for men to shave their hair during Umrah and Hajj. The Prophet, peace be upon him, called for the barber, who was Moimer Bin Abdullah, to have his head shaved. The believers present huddled around the Prophet, peace be upon him, trying to take his hair for blessings. When the barber started shaving the blessed head of the Prophet, peace be upon him, he himself distributed his hair amongst those present. Khalid bin Waleed took some of the hair of the Prophet, peace be upon him, and placed it in his cap. He would wear this during future battles and would always succeed when having the blessed hair of the Prophet, peace be upon him, with him.

On the 11th of Zil-Hajj (12th month of the Islamic calendar), Surah An-Nasr (Chapter of Help) Chapter 110) was revealed to the Prophet, peace be upon him. He, peace be upon him, knew that his time in the physical realm was coming to a close. He mounted on Qaswa and went to a place called Uqbah. This is where he would deliver his final sermon. This is where the Prophet, peace be upon him, stated that no Arab is superior to a non-Arab, nor are those who are black superior to those of colour, and vice versa, except piety. After the lengthy sermon, the Prophet, peace be upon him, went back to his tent and prayed the Zuhur and the Asr prayers. After the Hajj was finished, the Prophet, peace be upon him, returned to Madinah.

The passing of the Prophet (peace be upon him)

Around 2 weeks before the Prophet, peace be upon him, left this world, he started to feel quite ill. The Prophet, peace be upon him, started to have intense headaches and fevers. Although he was ill, he still kept leading the prayers at the Masjid in Madinah. During the illness, he split his time between the houses of his wives. He was first in the care of his wife, Hazrat Maimoonah, and then requested to be in the house of Hazrat Aisha. Over the course of the next few days or a week, the fever and headaches were getting more severe. Four days before the Prophet, peace be upon him, left this world, he appointed Hazrat Abu Bakr Siddique to lead the prayers as he was too weak to go to the mosque. Two days before his passing, the illness of the Prophet, peace be upon him, decreased. In the final moments of his physical life, the angel Jibraeel (Gabriel) approached the Prophet, peace be upon him, and asked how he was doing. The Prophet, peace be upon him, told him that he was in pain due to his illness. Then the angel of death (Angel Israeel) arrived; he sought the Prophet's peace upon his permission when entering the house and paid his upmost respect when conversing with him. The angel of death said to the Prophet peace be upon him that God has sent him to take his soul if he accepts, and if the angel of death doesn't have the Prophet peace be upon him's permission to take his soul, then the angel will go back, and the Prophet peace be upon him may remain on earth until he wishes. The Prophet, peace be upon him, gave the angel of death (Israeel) permission to take his soul away, which is what the angel of death did. As the Prophet, peace be upon him, was staying in the house of his wife Aisha, They both spent the last moments of his life together. Hazrat Aisha states that when the soul of the Prophet peace be upon him was taken away and ascended into the heavens, she smelt a fragrance that she had never smelt before.

The Prophet, peace be upon him, passed away on Monday in the month of Rabi-Ul-Awwal (3rd month in the Islamic calendar). Some say he passed away on the 27th or 28th of Safar (2nd month in the Islamic calendar). But his passing away in the month of Rabi-Ul-Awwal is more accurate. This is also the month in which the Prophet, peace be upon him, was born. He was also born on a Monday. He was 63 years old when he left the world.

The bathing of the Prophet, peace be upon him, was done by Hazrat Ali, Hazrat Usamah, and Hazrat Fazal Bin Abbas. In Islamic law, when washing the deceased, the body is to be covered, and water should go through the cloth, protecting their privacy. The grave of the Prophet, peace be upon him, was prepared by Hazrat Abu Ubaidah and Hazrat Abu Talha. The shroud of the Prophet, peace be upon him, was three white clothes made in a village in Yemen. Before the Prophet peace be upon him passed away, it was his will to leave his body near the grave alone for a while so people may visit him before they bury him. This will was fulfilled: first, the family members of the Prophet, peace be upon him, came to visit him, then the companions came after them to offer their condolences. The burial took place on Wednesday, as most early scholars of Islam have stated.

NOTE: The above biography is a very brief account of the life of the Prophet. Peace be upon him. The reason for not placing references above is due to the fact that every sentence would have had to be referenced. I didn't want to distract the audience by showing them evidence for the above accounts. I have primarily used the 7-volume work of Pir Karam Shah's work labelled "Zia-Un-Nabi" to write this short biography of the Prophet, peace be upon him. This is the most extensive and detailed Seerah (biography of the Prophet, peace be upon him) you will find in the English language. In that work, Pir Karam Shah has used the most authentic sources of the Prophet's life. If the audience wants to read a detailed account of the entire life of the Prophet, peace be upon him, and the conditions of the world before he was born and after he passed away, then please purchase a copy of Zia-Un-Nabi (the light of the Prophet, peace be upon him).

A physical description of the Prophet (peace be upon him)

The Prophet peace be upon him was neither too short nor tall; his skin complexion was fair, not too white nor too brown. His hair was neither too straight nor too curly. When the Prophet, peace be upon him, walked, he leaned forward slightly. He had a flat stomach and broad shoulders. His hair was fairly dense, and sometimes he would let it grow up to his shoulders. Sometimes his hair length was up to his earlobes, and sometimes his head was shaved completely. He had black pupils, long eyelashes, and large joints. He had a seal of Prophethood, which was between his shoulders. There was a slight gap between his front teeth, and every time he spoke, light appeared from it. The Prophet peace be upon him said those who have hair should honour it (Compilation of Abu Dawud). The Prophet peace be upon him would regularly oil his hair and comb his beard. There are various narrations about how many white hairs the Prophet, peace be upon him, had. Some companions say he had a few strands of grey hair; others say specifically he had 13 strands or 20 strands of grey hair. As human nature, this obviously changes throughout time. But what is certain is that he only had a few grey strands of hair. The Prophet, peace be upon him, would occasionally dye his hair with hennah (mehndi), which is typically used in South Asian culture. The Prophet, peace be upon him, would frequently use Kohl. Which is a black powder and is applied to the eyes to strengthen the eyesight and aid the growth of eyelashes. It's like a black eye liner. The Prophet, peace be upon him, would apply kohl to each eye three times before going to sleep. The Prophet, peace be upon him, would wear modest, loose clothing. Sometimes he wore red clothes more frequently; other times he would wear green clothing a lot, or white or black.

Throughout the life of the Prophet, peace be upon him, we can see that he never used to eat to his full and restricted certain types of foods. The sunnah for eating is to fill the stomach with 1/3 food, 1/3 water, and the other 1/3 empty. The sandals of the Prophet, peace be upon him, were made of leather, and each had two leather straps on top of them. The Prophet, peace be upon him, wore two ringers throughout his life. One of them was a silver ring with a black agate stone. The other ring was all silver, with a silver stone. The Prophet, peace be upon him, also had a third ring, which he would use to stamp letters. Some scholars say he didn't wear this ring and that it was only used for stamping purposes. The ring of the stamp had three lines on it, which said "Allah" on the first line, "Rasool" (Messenger) on the second line, and "Muhammad" on the third line. Like the picture below?

The Prophet peace be upon would usually wear a turban, not too big where it would be a burden on the head and not too small that it would not protect the head from cold and heat. The Prophet, peace be upon him, would usually wear a black turban. The companions would find it difficult to keep up with the Prophet, peace be upon him, when he was walking, as he would walk fast. Even when he walked at a normal pace, they would still find it difficult to keep up with him.

It is the practice of the Prophet, peace be upon him, to lick your fingers after finishing your meal. This is because the Prophet, peace be upon him, stated that you do not know which part of the food the blessing is contained in. One must use the right hand when eating, as the left hand is used for cleaning oneself when bathing and reviling oneself. Another benefit of licking the fingers after eating is that food is not wasted. The food consumed by the Prophet, peace be upon him, would usually be bread made with barley flour. He would abstain from eating red meat twice a day (though on rare occasions he did do this). Sometimes, he would have vinegar with his bread as a meal. It is a practice of all Prophets not to be fussy with food, as this is a blessing from Allah. There are many others around the world who live in starvation. Therefore, one should not complain about food; if you do not like a certain type of food, then one should avoid it without saying anything negative about it. The Prophet, peace be upon him, advised his nation to use olive oil in their food and to rub it on their bodies, as the olive tree is blessed in the religion of Islam. He used to enjoy eating pumpkin a lot. The benefits of pumpkins are that they sharpen the mind, cure headaches, and decrease thirst. The Prophet, peace be upon him, ate red meat such as cow, sheep, and lamb. He also ate chicken and rabbit. The Prophet, peace be upon him, had somewhat of a sweet tooth. He enjoyed eating fruits, in particular dates with cucumber and dates with watermelon. He, peace be upon him, enjoyed sweet and cold drinks. He used to like mixing honey, dates, or raisins with water. One of his favourite fruits was pomegranate.

The Prophet, peace be upon him, had a container that contained his perfume, which he would use. The Prophet, peace be upon him, never rejected three things: perfume, a pillow to rest on, and milk. The companions narrate that they never saw anyone smile more than the Prophet, peace upon him. Even after all the hardships he endured, he always saw the positive light in the issues he faced. Poetry was the media during the time of the Prophet, peace be upon him. The prophet, peace be upon him, would often recite poetry, as would his companions. Usually in praise of Allah and the final messenger.

Regarding the sleep of the Prophet, peace be upon him. When he would sleep, he would lay on his right side with his right hand under his right cheek. Before sleeping, the Prophet, peace be upon him, demonstrated the recitation of the last three chapters of the Quran.

1. Surah Ikhlas (Chapter of Sincerity) Also known as the chapter of Tawhid, meaning ones of Allah. The 112th

2. Surah Falaq (Chapter of the Daybreak, 113th chapter)

3. Surah Naas (Chapter of Mankind, 114th chapter)

He would recite these three chapters, blow on his hands, and then blow over his entire body. This is known to protect oneself from evil spirits and other harmful things.

The character of the Prophet, peace be upon him, was the humblest one could ever imagine. He dealt with so much abuse in his life that the only time he fought back was in battles. Hazrat Anas Ibn Malik served the Prophet, peace be upon him, for 10 years, and he never saw any negativity from the Prophet, peace be upon him. Not once did the Prophet peace be upon him complain about anything or be abusive to anyone, even though people were abusive to him. Hazrat Anas reports that the palm of the Prophet, peace be upon him, was the softest thing he ever touched, and he smelled nothing more beautiful than the fragrance of the Prophet, peace be upon him. The Prophet, peace be upon him, never responded to a bad deed with another bad deed; rather, he forgave those who hurt him. He was never verbally abusive to anyone. However, if the laws of Allah were broken by people, then he would become angry. An important note here is that he never got angry out of his ego; if he was angry, it would be that people have transgressed themselves from God, and he will always guide them back.

After the passing of the Prophet (peace be upon him)

After the Prophet, peace be upon him, left this world, Hazrat Abu Bakr Siddique was chosen to be the leader of the Muslims.

Chapter 10

Biographies of the Caliphs

Abu Bakr Siddique

Hazrat Abu Bakr Siddique was born in Makkah in the year 573. Making him 2-3 years younger than the Prophet, peace be upon him. He was also from the tribe of Quraysh, but from a different clan compared to the Prophet, peace be upon him. The Prophet, peace be upon him, was from Banu Hashim, and Abu Bakr was from Banu Taym. The real name of Abu Bakr was Abdullah. From a young age, he was always an honest and sincere person. Because of these traits, he was able to accompany the Prophet, peace be upon him, throughout his life due to the similarity in characteristics. Due to his human nature, even though alcohol was permitted at one point prior to Islam, early scholars say he did not indulge in liquor. He always helped those in need and helped others when going through difficulty. In the early stages of Islam, due to his wealth, he freed many slaves from oppression. He was a tradesman and would regularly accompany the Prophet, peace be upon him, for business visits. Due to his honesty and trustworthiness, people would leave their wealth with him if they needed a safe place to store it. His acceptance of Islam was done without any hesitation. He already knew the Prophet, peace be upon him, very well before declaring that he was a prophet. Due to their strong bond, Abu Bakr knew that the Prophet, peace be upon him, was the truthful messenger. He aided the Prophet, peace be upon him, in calling people to Islam in the early stages and throughout his life. During the most crucial times, split between life and death, Abu Bakr Siddique aided the Prophet, peace be upon him, during the migration to Madinah. The family of Abu Bakr supported the Prophet, peace be upon him, during this time when he was hiding in the cave of Thur (Ghar-e-Thur). The son and daughter of Abu Bakr would take them food and water to their hiding place.

One of the greatest efforts made by Hazrat Abu Bakr was the compilation of the Quran in book form. During the Prophets time, when revelation came, to preserve the words of God, they would be written on animal hide, stones, etc. Many companions memorised the Quran, and a lot were killed during the battles. This was the first edition of the Quran; during the reign of Harzat Umar Farooq and Hazrat Uthmaan, it would be further revised. The order of the Quran is not the order it was revealed in. The order of the Quran was set during the times of various caliphs. Abu Bakr didn't choose his family members to be governors of the public office for Muslims; rather, he chose those well-skilled for the job, as some may accuse him of financially benefiting from his reign as caliph. His cabinet ministers in Madinah were Hazrat Umar and Hazrat Ali, who were judges, and Hazrat Abu Ubaidah was the officer of the Treasury. Furthermore, Hazrat Abu Bakr established an Islamic law department to resolve any issues among Muslims. In the modern day and age, we would refer to them as "Shariah Councils.".

As well as a close friend, Abu Bakr was also the father-in-law of the Prophet, peace be upon him, as he married Aisha later in his life. An indication as to choosing Abu Bakr as his successor was when the Prophet, peace be upon him, gave Abu Bakr the responsibility of leading the Muslims to their first Hajj in the 9th year of Hijrah. After the passing of the Prophet, peace be upon him, in Masjid-e-Nabawai (Madinah), the people selected Abu Bakr to be the caliph and pledged their allegiance to him. Hazrat Abu Bakr faced numerous issues during his time as caliph; some of the Muslim tribes refused to pay their Zakat (mandatory tax to the poor), and some false claims arose about others being prophets, which he had to deal with. Before the passing of Abu Bakr, he proposed that Umar Farooq should be the next caliph. Most of the companions agreed to this, with the exception of Hazrat Ali and Hazrat Talha. According to early historians, it was on the 22nd Jamad-Ul-Akhir (6th Islamic month) in the 13th Hijrah that Abu Bakr passed away, aged 61, after being ill for around two weeks. His time as caliph lasted for two years, between the years 623 and 634.

Umar Farooq

The second caliph of Islam Hazrat Umar Farooq (also known as Umar Ibn Al-Khataab) was born in the year 583. He was also from the tribe of Quraysh. His title Al-Farooq (extinguisher) was given by the Prophet peace be upon, just as the Prophet gave the title of Siddique (truthful) to Hazrat Abu Bakr. The name Al-Farooq means distinguisher. Someone who distinguishes between good and evil. In his youth, he was known for his strength and for excelling in wrestling. Having the ability to read and write back in those days in Arabia was a unique gift, and he was one of those who were able to read and write. Just like the Prophet, peace be upon him, and Hazrat Abu Bakr, Hazrat Umar was also an entrepreneur. Before coming to Islam, he had married three times, and after converting to Islam, he had four wives. His first wife, Zainab, had three children with Hazrat Umar. Two sons, Abdullah and Abdul Rahman, and one daughter, Hafsa, who later in life married the Prophet, peace be upon him. Some of his wives didn't convert to Islam, so he divorced them.

Hazrat Umar, at one point, was strongly against Islam, to the point he set out to kill the Prophet, peace be upon him himself. One of his slave girls accepted Islam, and he physically abused her until she renounced her faith, which she refused. Hazrat Abu Bakr saw this and purchased her so she could be saved from the abuse. Even when he found out his own sister and brother-in-law converted to Islam, he became angry and abused them too, but they held strong to their faith. This was the moment Hazrat Umar changed his perspective on Islam. When he heard his sister and brother-in-law recite the Quran and lashed out, he felt guilty seeing the blood stains. He wanted to read what they were reciting, so after he lashed out, his sister Fatimah said he must take ablution when touching verses of the Quran. He went and washed himself, and written on the leaf was the beginning of Surah Ta-Ha, chapter 20 of the Quran. This is when he saw the beauty of the Quran and started to contemplate his stance on Islam. Later on, he approached the Prophet, peace be upon him, and accepted Islam at his hands. The people of Makkah were terrified of Hazrat Umar due to his strength and bravery. His conversion to Islam was a shock to the people of Makkah. As they say, the rest is history. Since his conversion, he has defended the Muslims in the battles and has been an asset to the Muslim world. During the migration of early Muslims, this was done in secrecy to prevent punishment. Being the brave person Umar Al-Farooq is, he openly announced that he would be migrating with the Muslims to Madinah, and if anyone dared, they should try to stop him. Which no one did due to the fear people had of him. Even though at one stage in his life he envied the Prophet, peace be upon him, he became one of his closest allies. The Prophet, peace be upon him, said that if there were to be a prophet after him, then it certainly would have been Hazrat Umar Al-Farooq. Hazrat Umar is a great example of how one's life can change with the right guidance. As consumption of liquor was popular across Arabia, Hazrat Umar used to consume large quantities of alcohol until the prohibition was revealed. This is an example we can use today, where so many are suffering from addiction. But once you're surrounded by the right people, Allah will open his doors for you.

During his reign, he established many Islamic institutes so people could learn the Quran and the teachings of the Prophet, peace be upon him. He also maintained the specialist Islamic law faculty that was left by Hazrat Abu Bakr. As the Islamic empire grew to parts of Turkey, other middle-eastern nations, and into Asia, To keep the law in order, Hazrat Abu Bakr formed a police force and established prisons. This was to ensure peace was being kept intact around the Muslim nations. To fund the Islamic movement further, as Zakaat was a necessity for Muslims only, he imposed a tax on non-Muslims to generate further revenue. The public funds would remain in a separate fund from the income received from Zakaat. With the public funds generated through other taxes, he would expand into new territories and pay workers to build roads and canals like he did with the Nile.

Even though he was a caliph and Islam had expanded vastly under his reign, he would often go out to the valleys and cities to see who was in need and support them as much as he could. When he saw people hungry, he would provide food and cooking ingredients for them. This would be regardless of their faith or colour. Similarly, for those disabled and unable to work, he provides some financial aid to them. As far as history can go, I believe this was first started by Hazrat Umar, and now many western countries provide financial aid to those who are disabled. The root for looking after and protecting civil rights was started by the Prophet, peace be upon him, and Muslims kept on developing it during their time as caliphs. Yet, western nations will take credit for this, even though it was started by Muslims. With any empire expansion, this also calls for an expansion of the army. Hazrat Umar reformed the military training, and soldiers had to know how to swim, ride animals, etc. With any expeditions within the army, he would send language translators and doctors so they could suffice themselves.

It was during the reign of Hazrat Umar that he conquered the Persian Empire as well as Jerusalem and other parts of the world. His reign over the Muslims lasted for 9–10 years, from 634–644. He was 61 years old when he passed away from the world. He was killed by a servant on the way to the mosque.

Uthmaan Ibn-Affaan

Hazrat Uthmaan was born in 573, making him 2-3 years younger than the Prophet, peace be upon him, and he was also from the Quraysh tribe. He embraced Islam during his early days of preaching. He is known as Dhun-Noorayn (possessor of the two lights), as he was the only companion honoured to marry two daughters of the Prophet, peace be upon him. His marriage was with Ruqayah. He then married Umme Kalthoom. He had a son with Ruqayah named Abdullah, who died in childhood. With Umme Kalthoom, he didn't have any children. After the passing of Umme Kalthoom, Hazrat Uthmaan married another eight times in total.

Historians and early Muslim scholars say he had 11 sons in total, with some dying in infancy. The number of daughters he had is uncertain; some say he had six, others say he had seven.

It was during the rule of Harzat Uthmaan that the Muslims established a navy force for the first time. This was due to the Byzantine Empire trying to overrule Syria and Cyprus. Hazrat Uthamaan's time allowed the Muslims to take control of Armenia and Azerbaijan. As the Muslim army expanded, some companions had control of certain armies in Muslim areas. Before planning an attack, they had to seek the permission of the current caliph. To strengthen Egypt further, the Muslims took over many parts of north Africa after north Africa was under Muslim control. Hazrat Uthmaan had set his eyes on expanding into Europe and taking over Spain. Although they didn't take over the whole of Spain, they managed to rule parts of it. By the year 711, all of Spain was under Muslim rule.

During the time of Hazraat Uthmaan, the copy of the Quran in book form was revised by him. As there are various dialects to recite the Quran, those who were non-Arab found it difficult to understand or even read the Quran. Therefore, he added grammatical rules to the Quran to make it easier to read. He was responsible for the first expansion of the Prophet's mosque (Masjid-e-Nabawi). As he was already a wealthy individual, he purchased the best materials around the world. He imported materials from India to construct the roof, as these were of the highest quality. He constructed a river around Madinah to prevent any floods. While he was the caliph of Islam, even though legally he was entitled to a salary, He did not take any money for himself but rather injected more of his own money to aid the Muslim government.

Hazrat Uthmaan made sure the Islamic caliphate was run strictly, just as the Prophet, peace be upon him, ran it. As well as Hazrat Abu Bakr and Hazrat Umar. However, his soft-hearted approach outweighed his anger. Hazrat Abu Bakr and Hazrat Umar were known for strictness. Nothing small passes them without taking action. However, Hazrat Uthmaan was different. He came across as rather gentle compared to his predecessors. The non-Muslims saw this as an advantage in that it may be possible to throw off his reign and try to defeat the Muslim army, or at least take over some of their land. Many Muslims were also worried by Hazrat Uthmaan's approach and saw it as a sign of weakness in Islamic leadership. Sometimes during his reign, there would be minor errors during the operation of the cabinet and office. With his soft approach and his workers getting away with light mistakes, they started to behave in a more rude way with Hazrat Uthmaan, even though he was their leader. Once those against Islam heard these stories, they created more rumours to dissect the unity of the Muslims. A Yemeni Jew by the name of Abdullah Ibn Saba was at the forefront of creating tales amongst the Muslims to cause friction amongst themselves. Ibn Saba became a false Muslim preacher; he took advantage of newly converted Muslims who had little knowledge and tried to throw them astray with his purposeful wrong interpretations of the Quran to dismantle the Muslims. He visited numerous Muslim cities but found Kufa in Iraq the best place to deviate Muslims off the right path. He represented himself as extremely pious and a dedicated follower of the Prophet, peace be upon him, but was a hidden Jew. He was summoned by the governor of Kufa and was removed from the city due to his propaganda. He eventually moved to Egypt, where he found much success in the false teachings of Islam. As his so-called group of new Muslims grew, they were indoctrinated by the poison Abdullah Ibn Saba spread to them. Thus believing that his version of Islam was genuinely the right path. This started becoming a severe problem amongst the Muslims as the followers of Abdullah Ibn Saba started to make false legal claims amongst Muslims, which resulted in Muslims facing punishment as the men of Abdullah Ibn Saba manipulated the Islamic legal system. They provided false witnesses and alibis to defend their story, making the public believe them.

This is where a conspiracy exists that the Shia sect was started by a Jew. Abdullah Ibn Saba and his army wanted Hazrat Ali to be caliph and believe he should have been caliph straight away after the Prophet peace be upon him passed. This is why they wanted Hazrat Uthmaan to step down from his position of power. Hazrat Ali refused to be caliph and didn't want any involvement with Abdullah Ibn Saba or his men.

After some time, Hazrat Uthmaan gathered his ministers to come up with a solution to the issue of Abdullah Ibn Saba. Some requested to go into battle with him. Hazrat Uthmaan rejected this idea to avoid further battles and people being killed. The main aim for the followers of Abdullah Ibn Saba was to remove Hazrat Uthmaan from his position as leader. Now that the false group of so-called Muslims grew well into the thousands, they forcefully surrounded the house of Hazrat Uthmaan. They requested he step down as caliph, but he rejected to do so, as he believes he was lawfully selected by the Muslims. They remained around his house for 40 days. They stopped and physically abused anyone who tried to take food or water into the house of Hazrat Uthmaan, who was held captive with his wife. He made it clear to the genuine Muslims not to attack the army of Abdullah ibn Saba, even those held hostage in his own house. Some of the men from Abdullah ibn Saba's army then forced entry into the house of Hazrat Uthmaan and murdered him. His wife tried to shield him but faced physical abuse herself. The sad reality is that the leaders of those who broke into the house of Hazrat Uthmaan (not all those surrounded by the house) broke in as there wasn't any need. Only a handful from the army broke in was Muhammad, the son of Hazrat Abu Bakr, that the Prophet peace be upon him dearly loved. Not only was Hazrat Uthmaan stabbed, but he was also beheaded by the thugs that broke in. Imam Hasan and Imam Hussain guarded the door of Hazrat Uthmaan so the men of Abdullah ibn Saba would not enter and harm Hazrat Uthmaan. They eventually jumped in through one of the windows, killing him off.

Once news broke out to the masses that Hazrat Uthmaan had been murdered, hell broke loose in Madinah. The mafia-style army of Abdullah Ibn Saba took over the public funds and stole as much as they could. The reign of Hazrat Uthmaan lasted 12–13 years. He took over in 644, after the killing of Hazrat Umar, until the year 656. The killing of Hazrat Uthmaan was indicated by the Prophet, peace be upon him, before he passed away. Once, when the Prophet peace be upon him, alongside Hazrat Abu Bakr, Hazrat Umar, and Uthmaan, stood on mount Uhud, he said, "Stand still, Uhud, there is a prophet, an honest man, and two martyrs" (Collection of Bukhari, Abu Dawood, and Tirmizi).

Ali Ibn Abi Taalib

According to some, Hazrat Ali (the cousin and son-in-law of the Prophet, peace be upon him) was either born in 599 or 600. So 29–30 years after the birth of the Prophet, peace be upon him. As he was a first cousin of the Prophet, peace be upon him, he was also from the Quraysh tribe and the same clan (Banu Hashim). He had three older brothers: Imam Jafar, Hazrat Aqil, and Hazrat Talib. He also had two sisters, Umme Hani and Jumana. Some historians say he had an additional brother by the name of Tulaiq and another sister called Raita. Hazrat Ali was unique in the sense that he was born inside the Kabah. He accepted Islam as a young boy and never worshipped any of the idols. Hazrat Ali was one of the closest people to the Prophet, peace be upon him, due to their relationship as cousins but also to his marrying the daughter of the Prophet, peace be upon him, Hazrat Fatima. They had five children together. Imam Hasan,

Imam Hussain, and Imam Mushin passed away as babies. He also had two daughters, Hazrat Zainab and Hazrat Umme Kalthoom.

Hazrat Ali was known for his fierce strength and bravery; he fought in all the battles since he reached maturity. He would often cause severe causalities for the opposition. When challenged to a fight, he never backed down and would always win. This is why Hazrat Ali is known as the lion of Allah.

Hazrat Ali, as well as being strong and courageous, is also known for his fountain of knowledge regarding Islam. The Prophet, peace be upon him, said, "I am the city of knowledge, and Ali is the door" (Mustadrak al-Hakim). He was eloquent in the Arabic language and was the root cause of Arabic syntax. As well as memorising the entire Quran, he was able to comment on every verse of the Quran uniquely. He had knowledge as to why and how every verse of the Quran was revealed. Just like his predecessors, he was cautious about how he ran his administration; he didn't indulge in public funds, nor did his family. Hazrat Ali improved the tax system of the time and introduced the land tax.

As Abdullah Ibn Saba's army killed off Hazrat Uthmaan, they can now put Hazrat Ali in power as they wanted. But he refused. He was already staying away from Abdullah Ibn Saba and his men, as he knew how evil their plot was. He didn't want to be appointed by them, as that made it look as if he was also against the administration of Hazrat Uthmaan, even though he wasn't. Even though he refused to be the 4th caliph, he eventually turned to the Muslims of Madinah, and the majority vote was for him to be the next caliph. This is what the genuine Muslims and Abdullah Ibn Saba's army wanted collectively. He agreed to be the 4th caliph of Islam. Now elected as leader, he got rid of the army of Abdullah Ibn Saba. As he knew they were mischievous, he told them to go back to their lands, which most did. Except for Abdullah Ibn Saba, he acted like he was a friend of Hazrat Ali and remained in Madinah. As the political situation was unstable, Hazrat Ali wanted to calm the situation and various parties down before hunting for the killers of Hazrat Uthmaan. Marwaan Ibn Hakam, who was working for the administration during Hazrat Uthmaan's time, was called to Hazrat Ali as he was present when the assassination of Hazrat Uthmaan took place. The other witness present at the time was the wife of Hazrat Uthmaan, who was Naylaah. As she was a housewife, she didn't leave the house much and was unable to recognise any of the killers except Muhammad, the son of Hazrat Abu Bakr. The son of Hazrat Abu Bakr denied killing Hazrat Uthmaan, saying he felt ashamed when Hazrat Uthmaan recognised him. Hazrat Ali was unsure of who was telling the truth and who was lying. The real Muslims during the time of Hazrat Uthmaan were also not keen on his leadership style and his cabinet members. Hazrat Ali decided to get rid of all them, as he knew this was an issue that was bothering the Muslims. To avoid further catastrophe, all of the current cabinet ministers appointed by Hazrat Uthmaan were removed from office. By now, Muslims owned land across Iraq, Afghanistan, Turkey, north Africa, parts of Pakistan (which was under India then), Syria, and more. Hazrat Ali selected new governors for these main hotspots. The previous governor of Syria was Muaawiyah under Hazrat Uthmaan. When Hazrat Ali sent the new governor of Syria, Muaawiyah rebelled and sent the new governor back to Madinah. This is when the conflict kept getting worse for the Muslim nation. Muaawiyah, the son of Abu Sufyan (the same Abu Sufyan that led numerous armies against the Prophet peace be upon him prior to his conversion to Islam), wanted to unite with the Muslims under Hazrat Ali's leadership only once justice was served for the murder of Hazrat Uthmaan.

The sun was setting on a new collision between the Muslims. Some companions went back to Makkah to inform Hazrat Aisha about the current condition of Madinah and how Hazrat Uthmaan was killed. They saw Hazrat Ali dealing with the situation lightly, so they took matters into their own hands. They prepared an army from Makkah led by Hazrat Aisha to deal with those responsible for killing Hazrat Uthmaan. Hazrat Aisha was on her way to Basra, Iraq, with her army. There, more recruits of the same ideology joined forces. They ended up overthrowing Basra and capturing the governor, who was looking after that region on behalf of the Islamic empire at the time (a deputy of Hazrat Ali). Things were starting to get worse. Hazrat Ali set off for Basra to try to cool the situation and did not approach Hazrat Aisha's army to fight. Some companions didn't join Hazrat Ali as they thought he was delaying the process of capturing the killers of Hazrat Uthmaan. This meant he lost more followers, and they sided with the army of Hazrat Aisha. On the way to Basra, Hazrat Ali was accompanied by Abdullah Ibn Saba, who was portraying himself as a pious Muslim even though he was a Jew. Abdullah Ibn Saba sent men in secrecy to tell the people of Basra that Hazrat Ali was on his way to take the Muslims as prisoners for overthrowing the Basra state, which was under the Islamic caliphate (under the leadership of Hazrat Ali), and that they should fight back. When Hazrat Ali approached Basra, he assured them of peace and told his army not to fight under any circumstances. But the conniving plan of Abdullah Ibn Saba turned up the heat. Abdullah Ibn Saba and his followers launched an attack on the army of Hazrat Aisha. Full chaos has now erupted; everyone is playing a blame game. That night, thousands of Muslims were killed fighting each other. After the fighting was stopped, the people of Basra accepted Hazrat Ali as the caliph.

After seeing more bloodshed take place in Madinah, where thousands of Muslims died fighting each other due to the troubles and tales caused by Abdullah Ibn Saba, Hazrat Ali decided to leave Madinah so the city could be in peace and made Kufa in Iraq the new capital of the Muslim empire. Hazrat Ali attempted peaceful negotiations with Muaawiyah, who had kept himself as governor of Syria, to unite the Muslims once again. To anger and frustrate Muslims, Muaawiyah held the shirt that was worn by Hazrat Uthmaan when he was killed, covered in blood, and his amputated fingers on display in Damascus. The Muslims of Syria wanted revenge for the murder of Hazrat Uthmaan. As Hazrat Ali had expelled the majority of the army of Abdullah Ibn Saba once he came into power, his notion was that it would be impossible to find the killers of Hazrat Uthmaan as they would've gone way too far to find them. Other Muslims disagreed, so they partnered with Muaawiyah and Hazrat Aisha's armies. This disagreement, along with Muaawiyah refusing to pledge allegiance to Hazrat Ali, led to the battle of Siffin in the year 657 (the 37th Hijrah). Deep down, neither Hazrat Ali nor Muaawiyah wanted this fight to happen, as it was Muslims fighting Muslims. But there seemed to be no other way to solve this issue, according to them. The battle (the Battle of Siffin) lasted for a few days, and around 80,000 Muslims from both sides died. Up until then, this was the worst catastrophe for Muslims. Even after all the lives lost in the battle of Siffin, there was still no resolution between Hazrat Ali and Muaawiyah.

Hazrat Ali was killed on his way to the Fajr prayer in Kufa, Iraq. Three people were responsible for his assassination. They dipped their swords into poison and struck Hazrat Ali on the head. This occurred on Friday 17th Ramadan (Some say 19th or 21st of Ramadan.

Chapter II

Biographies of the 4 Imams

Introduction

This chapter will cover brief biographies of the four imams of Islamic law. Imam Abu Hanifah, Imam Shafi, Imam Malik, and Imam Ahmed Ibn Hanbal. We will also cover the necessity as to why Muslims must follow at least one of the Imams and the consequences to one's faith when not following a Mazhab (school of thought).

The importance of following a school of thought (Mazhab)

Islam is a vast religion, with numerous rules and regulations for pretty much every problem one can encounter in life or difficulty communities may face. Although knowledge is a click away in the era of technology, our knowledge is little compared to that of early Muslim scholars. The 4 Imams established the schools of thought and set the guidelines of Islam, making it easy for common people like us to follow. Even the greatest of Islamic scholars followed a school of thought. Our interpretations of religion will be picked and followed according to our evil desires. The 4 Imams set out a blueprint for the interpretations of Islamic rulings due to the oceans of knowledge they contained. With their teachings, it makes Islam an easier religion to follow. This is also the beauty of Islam, as it caters to anyone and everyone. If one does not follow a school of thought, they will end up in confusion and not knowing how to go about religious practices. It is important to note that these 4 Imams held different opinions, and one is not right and the other is not wrong. The 4 Imams cater to the various lifestyles of Islam, and one should choose the school of thought best matched to them. For example, there were times when the Prophet peace be upon him prayed and he would raise his hands after standing from the Ruku position, while sometimes he didn't do this. So which method is right? As Muslims, we cannot pick and choose what we want to follow; we must adhere to one method. This is where the four imams play a crucial role. Following one of their methods brings consistency in worship and gives Muslims a framework for religious principles. The 4 Imams derived Islamic rulings based on the exegesis of the Quran and their knowledge of Hadith (sayings and actions of the Prophet, peace be upon him). They were experts in numerous Islamic scholarly fields and were not just restricted to one Islamic science. When one faces issues in life or religious worship, they can turn to their opinions to derive a conclusion about the matter. For example, if a Muslim is going through a divorce, What is the correct Islamic ruling on this, and how should they overcome it? It's not as simple as saying that the married couple do not get along and that they are just going to press the exit button. A lot of formalities have to take place. Furthermore, it brings a sense of community and tradition to the Islamic religion. This is why, in certain parts of the world, one school of thought will have more followers than another school of thought. For example, across South Asia, the Hanafi method of Imam Abu Hanifa is followed more than other schools of thought. As they have a history of following the opinion of Imam Abu Hanifa, it will allow society to unite and function more smoothly as literally everyone is following the same method of Islamic law, making it easier for Islamic judges (Mufti's) to give rulings in their communities. Whereas, if you go to East Asia, most of the countries and people follow the Shafi school of thought of Imam Shafi.

One primary advantage of following a madhhab is the clarity it offers in navigating the complexities of Islamic jurisprudence. With four major Sunni madhhabs—Hanafi, Maliki, Shafi'i, and Hanbali—each has its own unique methodologies and interpretations derived from the Quran and Hadith. By aligning with a specific madhhab, a Muslim gains a comprehensive and systematic approach to religious teachings, making it easier to understand and implement the principles of Islam in daily life.

Consistency in religious practices is another crucial aspect of following a madhhab. Islamic law covers various aspects of life, from personal rituals to social and economic matters. Different madhhabs may have varying opinions on certain issues, and adhering to a specific school of thought provides a consistent approach to these diverse aspects. This consistency ensures that Muslims can approach their religious obligations with confidence, knowing that their actions align with the principles of their chosen madhhab. Furthermore, following a madhhab simplifies the decision-making process for individuals. Islamic jurisprudence can be intricate and nuanced, requiring a deep understanding of religious texts and traditions. By aligning with a madhhab, individuals can rely on the expertise of scholars within that school to guide them in making informed decisions. This reliance on established principles and scholarship aids in avoiding subjective interpretations and potential misunderstandings of religious teachings.

Imam Abu Hanifah (founder of the Hanafi school of thought)

Imam Abu Hanifah was born in the year 699 (the 80th Hijrah) in Kufa, Iraq. His full name was Abu Hanifa Al-Numaan Bin Thaabit. He came from what is known by early historians as a wealthy background due to the travels his father took, who was a businessman who predominantly traded silk clothing. When Imam Abu Hanifah was a child, his father took him to Hazrat Ali to bless the children. Although he was of Persian descent, from a young age he grasped the Arabic language extremely well. During his early years, he memorised the Quran, understood its commentary, and learned the sayings of the Prophet, peace be upon him (Hadith). Once he got into the family trade, he became known for his honesty and positive characteristics. Imam Abu Hanifah excelled in his various Islamic sciences, in particular theology and Islamic law. One of his notable teachers who was popular at that time in Kufa was Hammad Ibn Sulaymaan. He then left Kufa to study in Makkah for around 6 years. He had teachers in the thousands at this stage as she studied various branches of Islam from specialised tutors. Out of the 4 Imams, Imam Abu Hanifah was the only one to live and learn amongst the companions of the Prophet, peace be upon him. This is why Imam Abu Hanifah is known as a Tabiee (someone who saw the companions of the Prophet, peace be upon him, but not the Prophet, peace be upon himself). Which is the most followed out of the four imams around the world? He is known to adapt Islamic rulings to the current social context. In the modern era of technology, it is close to impossible to live just as the Prophet, peace be upon him, lived. His method was a development of Islam. As the world kept changing from the time of the Prophet, peace be upon him, he and the other 3 Imams of Islamic law managed to find solutions for Muslims and keep them firm in their faith whilst dealing with various social issues.

Once Imam Abu Hanifah was 40 years old, he replaced his teacher, Hammad Ibn Sulaymaan. He offered many religious verdicts and was able to give solutions to those facing issues in society. As he was able to find practical solutions due to his emphasis on analogical reasoning, he went on to establish the Hanafi school of thought. He was already from a well-off family financially, and he himself entered the family business and was fairly wealthy. The people of Kufa knew that he wasn't distracted by the greed of money or power. This is why they saw him as most suitable to be a judge, alongside his vast knowledge of Islam. Over time, his number of students grew, who were also equipped with the same depth of knowledge of Islam as he was. He would regularly consult with a board of 40 students when giving Islamic verdicts to gain their opinion. Two of his students outshone others. They are Imam Abu Yusuf and Imam Mohammed. They were knowledgeable enough to start their own school of thought but didn't see the need to. One of the requirements Imam Abu

Hanifah had to meet to be accepted as a student was to memorise the Quran. This can be seen as somewhat of a dedication to the religion and the seriousness of learning the religion. This also had the ability for students to be diligent when giving Islamic verdicts, as they had memorised the root source. He further funded his students who were not in a good financial state. For those students who came from poorer backgrounds, he would leave them bursaries, as he didn't want money to be the cause of students not continuing with their education. The financial aid led students to live and eat while focusing on their education. Imam Abu Hanifah saw the talent of his students and knew they would be a future influence. By offering his financial assistance, he knew they could fully focus on their studies and gain more knowledge of the sciences of Islam.

Once the knowledge of Imam Abu Hanifah grew, so did his popularity. He was known for his Islamic legal rulings. Unfortunately, the Islamic caliphate at the time had significantly changed from what the Prophet, peace be upon him, left behind. The Islamic governors at the time were living lavish lifestyles in palaces rather than being people of the masses like their predecessors. The caliphate at the time wanted Imam Abu Hanifah to be a chief judge, but he refused as he did not agree with those in power who were abusing true Islamic rulings. As he kept rejecting their offer, he was sent to prison and received 110 lashes over the course of 11 days. Due to this suffering, he passed away in the year 767 (the 150th Hijrah). He was buried in present-day Baghdad, and his tomb is visited by numerous followers paying their respects.

Imam Maalik (founder of the Maaliki school of thought)

Imam Maalik Ibn Anas was born in 711 in Madinah. From a young age, he was in the association of prominent scholars of Madinah at the time. This is where he learned the religion holistically. He gained an understanding of Islamic law and the commentary of the Quran and Hadith. His most famous work is "Muwatta." In this book, he collected numerous sayings of the Prophet, peace be upon him, and how they can be used for Islamic legal practices. He relied on the practices of the people of Madinah, as he believed they embedded the knowledge of the Prophet, peace be upon him, in their daily aspects of life, whether it be family, socialising with the community, or even business matters. He studied under at least 900 scholars. Imam Maalik had a sharp memory, which allowed him to memorise the sayings of the Prophet, peace be upon him, at a quicker pace compared to most. Since the age of 17, he has started to teach the sayings of the Prophet (peace be upon him) and Islamic law, as well as give religious verdicts on an array of matters. Imam Maalik had immense love for the Prophet, peace be upon him, even though he physically didn't see him. Out of respect, he would walk barefoot in Madinah, as it is the resting place of the Prophet. Peace be upon him. The house Imam Maalik stayed in in Madinah was the house of Abdullah Ibn Masood, who was a well-known companion of the Prophet, peace be upon him.

He passed away in the year 795 in Madinah.

Imam Shafi (founder of the Shafi school of thought)

His full name was Abu Abdullah Muhammad Ibn Idris Ash-Shafi. He was born in Gaza, Palestine, in the year 767. His father passed away during his childhood, and he was raised by his mom and extended family members. By the age of 7, he had also memorised the Quran. He studied in Makkah, and when he was around 20 years of age, he left for Madinah to learn from Imam Maalik himself. This is where he gained a detailed understanding of the Maliki school. After his studies in Madinah, he headed to Iraq to upskill in Islamic law and the sayings of the Prophet, peace be upon him (Hadith). After compiling all this knowledge, this laid the foundation for him to establish the Shafi school of thought. One of his most famous works is known as "Al-Risala," where he outlines the principles of Islamic law (jurisprudence) and legal theory. This work strongly emphasises the use of evidence from the original source (the Quran and Hadith) and analysing its reasonings to drive legal rulings. He passed away in the year 820 in Cairo, Egypt. He is buried in the Mosque of Al-Shafi (Masjid Shafi), where his tomb is.

Imam Ahmed Ibn Hanbal
(founder of the Hanbali school of thought)

Imam Ahmed was born in 780 in Baghdad, Iraq. He came from a religious family, and one of his first teachers was his mother, who was well-versed in Islamic sciences. He studied in Baghdad under Imam Shafi, who heavily influenced his development. He was more strict in preserving authentic sayings of the Prophet, peace be upon him, and wouldn't compromise any external factors in his judgements, such as politics. As he was quite strict in his legal rulings compared to the other three imams (even though they are not wrong), he faced numerous trials as he refused to accept the rulings of governors at the time. He was imprisoned numerous times due to his refutations. His most popular work is known as the "Musnad of Imam Ahmed Ibn Hanbal," where he compiled around 40,000 hadith. He chose this 40,000 out of 750,000 hadiths that he knew. This goes to show how much research and how broad the knowledge of Imam Ahmed was.

He passed away in the year 855.

Chapter 12

Spiritual Refinement

This book is targeted at new Muslims, those interested in Islam, or those who have been Muslims for a long time or since birth. The concept of spiritually refining oneself is the essence of faith. Without spirituality, you're just a body performing rituals, when in reality those rituals are spiritual. For example, anyone can pray five times a day. But how many can pray five times a day with full focus? Without their minds and hearts travelling to numerous places, when should your heart and mind be present in the prayer? Or even when one is fasting. The easy part is to refrain from food and drink. But while fasting, how do you protect your heart and mind from negative thoughts? Unfortunately, the majority of Muslims in modern times turn a blind eye to spiritual practices. They have fallen into the trap of the devil and their ego and think they do not need any spirituality. What does a Muslim do in between the five daily prayers? How do you keep yourself conscious of Allah? These are questions one can only understand once they have grasped the spiritual concept of Islam. I am of the opinion that no one can taste the sweetness of faith until they have gone through a spiritual journey. For those who have converted to or are interested in Islam, You will certainly reach a state where things have plateaued. Those who have been Muslim for a while will know exactly what I am talking about. For example, if you have converted to Islam for a few months or maybe even a few years, you will feel spiritually elevated, something I call the "honeymoon phase." This will eventually fizzle out. Your worship will not have the same effect on you as when you started. Especially when and if life starts getting a bit hard. This is why spiritual practices exist in Islam, and those who seek spirituality keep tasting the sweetness of faith. Only it keeps getting sweeter and sweeter due to their practices. For example, recite the names of Allah in between prayers a certain number of times. Or, reciting praises and prayers (Durood Shareef) on the Prophet, peace be upon him, a certain number of times every day. Over time, if you keep increasing the daily count, you will feel more spiritually elevated as time goes by. However, in Islamic history, those who have mastered the concept of spirituality only mastered it with the help of a spiritual teacher (Murshid). It is impossible to reach spiritual states by oneself. Only prophets can do that. The companions took the Prophet, peace be upon him, as their teacher; those who came after the companions took the companions as their teachers; and it goes on and on and will continue until the day of judgement. The concepts of spirituality may be found in books, but you will never understand them until you yourself step on the path. No human except Prophets is perfect, so the journey of spiritual refinement never really stops. But, over time, you can and will get closer to Allah.

In modern times, these practices can be known as Sufism. But unfortunately, the term Sufism or Sufi has been tarnished by fraudulent people claiming to be spiritual guides. When people see certain actions in the name of Sufism, they automatically think all Sufis are misguided. This is a negative mentality. It is the same as saying all Muslims are terrorists just because one so-called Muslim decided to carry out an act of terror. Other names for Sufism are "Ihsaan," which means excellence. It can be "Tazkiyah-Tun-Nafs(purification of the self) or Tassawuf (Sufism or Islamic mysticism). Just because one person may be a scholar doesn't mean they are spiritual. Scholars can still have ill thoughts. For example, looking at someone lustfully, they may lie or tell tales between two people or two groups. This is something people shouldn't be fooled by. It's like a doctor not being ethical in their practices. Although they are educated and in positions of power and authority, that doesn't mean they have the answers to everything related to their field. Pure spirituality cannot be learned from books and definitely not from the Internet, although you may find useful blueprints. When seeking knowledge, you should strive and attend classes to gain the full blessing. The physical classroom is a lot different compared to the Internet. You will absorb more knowledge and have full interaction with the teacher to tackle any difficulties that may occur. This is the real method of gaining knowledge. The companions sat with the Prophet, peace be upon him, to learn and soak in what he was saying, and this is the traditional method. The elite scholars of the past and present left their towns, cities, and even countries to find the beauty of Islam. Do not expect it to come to your door. It's like money; we have to go and work for it; it doesn't come automatically to us.

The spiritual masters in Islam are known as the "Awliyah" (friends of Allah). This is clearly mentioned in the Quran, as Allah says:

Translation: *"There will certainly be no fear for the close servants of Allah, nor will they grieve."*
(Surah Yunus, Verse 62)

They are known as the friends of Allah, has they have worshipped Allah immensely whilst burning away their ego. The Prophet peace be upon him states:

On the authority of Abu Hurayrah (may Allah be pleased with him), who said that the Messenger of Allah (ﷺ) said: Allah (mighty and sublime be He) said: Whosoever shows enmity to someone devoted to Me, I shall be at war with him. My servant draws not near to Me with anything more loved by Me than the religious duties I have enjoined upon him, and My servant continues to draw near to me with supererogatory works so that I shall love him. When I love him I am his hearing with which he hears, his seeing with which he sees, his hand with which he strikes and his foot with which he walks. Were he to ask [something] of me, I would surely give it to him, and were he to ask Me for refuge, I would surely grant him it. I do not hesitate about anything as much as I hesitate about [seizing] the soul of My faithful servant: he hates death and I hate hurting him. It was related by al-Bukhari.

Some of the most renowned amongst the Awliyah/spiritual masters (Murshids) in Islamic history are:

- Hazrat Abdul Qadir Jilani is from Baghdad, Iraq (1078–1166). Who founded the Qadri order.

- Hazrat Khawja Moin Uddin Chisti. Some say he was born in Nishapur, Iran; others say he was born in Sistaan, Iran (1143–1236). During his journey to Hajj, he saw the Prophet, peace be upon him, in a spiritual vision where he was ordered to go to Ajmer, India, to propagate Islam. It is said he converted around 9 million people to Islam through his teachings. He is the founder of the Chistiyya order and is buried in Ajmer, India.

- Hazrat Shah-Jalal Yemeni (1271–1346) Hazrat Shah Jalal is most famous for conquering Sylhet, Bangladesh. On the instruction of his spiritual master and uncle Shah Ahmed Kabir, he was given a handful of soil and was tasked with travelling until he reached a destination that matched the colour, fragrance, and texture of that soil. Some say he travelled from Yemen; others say he travelled from Turkey. On his journey, he gained followers of 360 disciples, who, under his guidance, became spiritual masters themselves. Hazrat Shah Jalal is responsible for the mass conversion of Bangladesh, and the Sylhet region in particular, after battling Hindu tribes. It is due to his efforts that the people of Bangladesh are Muslim.

- Hazrat Baha-Uddin Naqshbandi (1318–1389) He is the founder of the Naqshbandi order, which is one of the most popular Sufi traditions.

- Hazrat Abul Hasan Shadhili (1196–1258) Born in Morocco, he travelled around many places in the world, with his final resting place in Egypt. He is the founder of the Shadhili path.

I have only named a few to give you an example. There are numerous historic saints in Islamic history. With a lot of them being based across Asia, One may ask why Asia is the home of a lot of Awliyah (saints or sages—friends of Allah). If you look at the history of these countries, a lot of them diverted from Islam and were in desperate need of a saviour. Someone who can guide them back to Allah and his Prophet, peace be upon him. Especially in South Asia and East Asia, where idol worshipping and fire worshipping were still big concerns, Allah chose these people to dedicate their lives to spreading Islam. Endless books can be written on the saints. Unfortunately, narrow-minded Muslims think Sufism is only a concept in Asia. That is wrong. Although some of the practices that take place at Sufi shrines are forbidden, such as stupid people prostrating to the saints or performing Tawaf around the graves of the saints, They are automatically under the impression that the saints resting there were also transgressors of Islam, but that is not true. If someone has passed away centuries ago and forbidden actions take place at their burial site, what do you expect them to do? They can't physically come back to life and put a stop to it, can they? Most of the prominent Awliyah are Sayyids (descendants of the Prophet, peace be upon him). This is one of the reasons why they can reach high spiritual stations and gain closeness to Allah just by having the blood of the Prophet, peace be upon him, in them.

The readers shouldn't get confused about these orders they founded with the Imams of the school of thought, as discussed earlier. The four imams, such as Imam Abu Hanifa, Imam Shafi, Imam Maalik, and Imam Ahmed Ibn Hambal, have laid the foundations for Islamic law. The Awliyah have laid the foundations for the remembrance of Allah (Zikr). The Sufi tradition is that they must follow one of the four imams. For example, you can be a Hanafi or Shafi and still be a Naqshbandi disciple. The difference between the Sufi paths (Tariqah's) is the rhythm when it comes to Zikr. Various paths, such as the Naqshbandi, Qadriyah, Chistiyyah, and so forth, all have the same goal. Bringing people closer to Allah through his remembrance. Certain Sufi paths will chant particular names of Allah for a certain amount of time (Tasbeeh), compared to others. This is the only difference. All the Sufi paths have very similar creeds; for example, they believe the Prophet peace be upon him is light, unlike some who claim he is just a "normal" human being. Just because he had a physical presence does not mean he is a normal man. When he used to sweat, the fragrance of musk would strongly smell from him. This is obviously not the case with any other human. So how and why do people think it's ok to degrade the Prophet, peace be upon him, in this manner? It makes no sense and is out of their own ignorance. The main emphasis is all on the remembrance of Allah and for followers to get closer to him as well as to the Prophet, peace be upon him. There are approximately 41 different Sufi paths (Tariqah's). Some are even branched off other Tariqah's or Silsila's.

Silsila means chain (chain of teachers). The founder of all the Sufi chains is the Prophet; peace be upon him. He taught his family (Ahlul-Bayt) and the companions in numerous ways; they then passed this knowledge of spirituality to their students, and their students have continued to do so to this day. Another difference between the Sufi path's is the syllabus that gets taught to the student. For example, in the Naqshbandi way, the spiritual mentor (Murshid) may tell his disciples (Mureeds) to recite the name of Allah 100 times a day on a prayer bead (Tasbeeh). A spiritual mentor of the Qadriyah path may tell the disciples to read the name of Allah 50 times and to send salutations to the Prophet, peace be upon him, 50 times. This is only an example.

There are many sub-branches of each silsila (chain). Think of it this way. If you are a teacher with 100 students, You may need to alter your teaching methods to cater for the entire 100 students, as we all perceive knowledge in various ways. Those 100 students will go out and teach other batches of students the same method; they learned it from their teacher and may explain it in a different way. Although the root knowledge and purpose are the same, the teachings get altered slightly. This is the same with the paths of spirituality. Some groups may hold gatherings of zikr (remembrance of Allah). Some of the names out of the 99 names of Allah are chanted in a loud setting. In addition to sending numerous salutations to the Prophet, peace be upon him, That's literally the only difference. Some may do this standing, which is known as Hadrah in Sufi terms, but most will do this while seated, as Allah says in the Quran:

$$ٱلَّذِينَ يَذْكُرُونَ ٱللَّهَ قِيَـٰمًا وَقُعُودًا وَعَلَىٰ جُنُوبِهِمْ وَيَتَفَكَّرُونَ فِى خَلْقِ ٱلسَّمَـٰوَٰتِ وَٱلْأَرْضِ رَبَّنَا مَا خَلَقْتَ هَـٰذَا بَـٰطِلًا سُبْحَـٰنَكَ فَقِنَا عَذَابَ ٱلنَّارِ$$

Translation: ⌈They are⌉ those who remember Allah while standing, sitting, and lying on their sides, and reflect on the creation of the heavens and the earth ⌈and pray⌉, "Our Lord! You have not created ⌈all of⌉ this without purpose. Glory be to You! Protect us from the torment of the Fire. (Surah Al-Imran, Verse 191)

On the authority of Abu Hurayrah (may Allah be pleased with him), who said that the Prophet (ﷺ) said: Allah the almighty said: I am as my servant thinks I am. I am with him when he makes mention of me. If he makes mention of me to himself, I make mention of him to myself; and if he makes mention of me in an assembly, I make mention of him in an assembly better than it. And if he draws near to me an arm's length, I draw near to him a cubit, and if he draws near to me a cubit, I draw near to him a fathom. And if he comes to me walking, I go to him at speed.

Another possible rendering of the Arabic is: "I am as my servant expects me to be". The meaning is that forgiveness and acceptance of repentance by the almighty is subject to His servant truly believing that He is forgiving and merciful. However, not to accompany such belief with right action would be to mock the Almighty. It was related by al-Buhkari (also by Muslim, at-Tirmidhi and Ibn-Majah).

When someone decides to be a disciple (Mureed) of a genuine spiritual master (Murshid), The tasks will slowly increase as your spiritual state improves. If you start off reading one portion of the Quran out of the 30 portions, The teacher may start telling you to recite two portions of the Quran now. You keep improving, and there's no end. Because we are not perfect beings, there is always room for improvement. The more you improve, the closer you become to Allah and his Prophet, peace be upon him. Many people on these paths start to sense the Prophet, peace be upon him, and can eventually see him. This is the aim of Sufi traditions: to cleanse oneself and be pure. The purpose is to destroy your ego and burn negative emotions such as jealousy, lust, greed, spitefulness, etc. This can only be done through the remembrance of Allah and his Prophet, peace be upon him. The more one remembers Allah, the less chance there is for evil to be within you, as you will be busy calling upon Allah when being guided by a spiritual master.

Sufism has never been more important today than ever. With all the evil around us, a genuine spiritual mentor will have the ability to pull his disciples away from the mess we live in. Everything is sexualized, which has increased openness and fornication in society. People struggle to find the meaning of life. Sufism combats all these issues. It makes you realise that you're not even a drop in the ocean of creation, thus knocking the arrogance and ignorance out of oneself. How many people do we see showing off on social media? It's pure arrogance. There is always someone better than you out there in the world. Whether it's physical looks, wealth, happiness, and the list goes on, Sufism teaches followers not to be selfish and to honour all of God's creation. Not to look at someone and think you are better than them. This is against the teachings of the Prophet, peace be upon him. Sufism teaches you to connect to humankind and to serve those who are in less fortunate positions than us. There are many Sufi lodges in the west, where they have established hostels to feed the poor and shelter the homeless. This is what Sufism is all about. It's to practice the Sunnah of the Prophet, peace be upon him, to the best of one's ability. Always be humble, soft-hearted, and have a gentle approach. Unfortunately, there are too many scholars in the world, especially on social media, where they come across as arrogant, foul-mouthed, and hot-headed. This is not the way of the Prophet; peace be upon him. He, peace be upon him, never belittled anyone; he never made anyone feel guilty for not practicing the faith; he never forced anyone to accept faith. He used his humble approach, beautiful manners, and character to make people fall in love with Islam. This is the Sunnah the Awliyah have carried with them and have instilled in their followers. The problem for many new converts and reverts to Islam is that they have been sucked into the ideology of Wahhabism and Salafism. The Salafi group claims to live their lives according to the early generation of Muslims, which is clearly not practical as the world has drastically changed since then. Wahhabism was forced upon western governments in Saudi Arabia to cause disunity among Muslims. When Muslims around the world are united, you have revolutions such as the Ottoman Empire, which ruled for over 600 years. Western governments know they can't afford for these strong Muslim empires to rule parts of the world, as western governments cannot benefit from these empires. The Ottoman Empire was based on Sufi principles. The west, in particular the UK and USA, broke down the Ottomans and placed the king in Saudi Arabia as a gateway for them to access resources. Over the past century, narrow-minded Muslims have fallen into the trap of Wahhabism and have the mentality that "if the Arabs do it, then that must be right as the Prophet was an Arab." This is not true. You will be surprised at how many Arab-speaking people cannot understand the Quran. The Quran is in classical Arabic. It's like learning Shakespeare and thinking it's modern English when it isn't. Those interested in Islam or who have converted should be aware of this. Wahhabism and Salafism are what create radicals and then shame the entire religion of Islam. When have you ever heard of a Sunni Muslim committing an act of terror and killing innocent people? All Sufi groups fall under the Sunni sect. If you classify yourself as a Sunni, then there are other precise sub-groups. A Sunni Muslim will always adopt one of the four schools of law.

Some may say, Aren't the Quran and the five daily forms the best forms of Zikr? The answer is yes. But we are still in need of a spiritual guide. It's easy to recite the Quran yourself, but to understand it and implement it, you need a teacher. When we fall ill, we visit the doctor. Similarly, with our spiritual diseases of lust, greed, anger, jealousy, arrogance, and more, we must go to someone who can help us get rid of these negative traits. This is how your quality of worship improves, and there's a higher chance your prayers will be answered by Allah as you will be in a cleaner spiritual state. Remember how the first mandatory act of prayer is to clean one's body? If the body is made of two elements, the soul and the physical body, It's easy to wash the physical body, but what about the inner state? How does one clean the heart and soul? So many Muslims now prostrate to Allah with arrogance in their hearts, thinking they are better than others. Do you really think Allah likes these qualities? And then to have the courage to stand before him and prostrate to him with that inner dirt inside you? This is the blessing we have; the Awliyah have taken it from their teachers, who took it from their teachers, going all the way back to the Prophet, peace be upon him, and equipping themselves with these skills to benefit the Muslims. But no one really wants to believe in spiritual guides. Muslims think they can reach God's presence all on their own. That's totally wrong. If that were the case, there's no need for prophets. There's no need for the angel Gabriel (Jibraeel) to come to deliver the message, as Allah is more than capable of doing it himself. There always has to be an intermediary. You cannot knock on the door of the president or prime minister without having a connection that leads you there. Thinking to yourself that you're not in need of a guide is the trap of the devil. When facing issues, who do you consult with? The guidance of a spiritual master is different from what a regular imam will tell you, and it certainly is different from what your friends and family will say. A genuine spiritual guide will not talk for their own benefit. They will always include other aspects when making a decision when you consult them, as they are spiritual doctors. The Imam may give you the answer of a one-size-fits all approach. Your friends and family may have inner ill thoughts in them and may give you an answer on what's best for themselves and not for you. This is how Muslims are supposed to improve themselves over time. By having a true guide who can not only guide them through life obstacles but also on their spiritual journey.

The requirements of a true Murshid. Is one who is learned in the sciences of Islam, such as Islamic law (Jurisprudence), the studies of Hadith, the recitation of the Quran (Qiraat), and so forth. This basically equivalates with a qualified religious scholar. The necessity of spiritual sciences such as Sufism and Tasswauf is that one has a strong foundation in the knowledge of the Shariah. It is impossible to spiritually exceed oneself without having knowledge of Allah and his Messenger, peace be upon him. For example, how can one perfect their inner state if there are errors in their prayer or fasting? To make sure you are praying and fasting according to the correct methods, you must first follow its rules and regulations. Thus, with an educated spiritual guide, he will be able to guide you in religious matters. The spiritual guide will obviously have a spiritual mentor himself who has walked the path of spirituality himself under his guide and has freed himself from evil vices. How can one guide you on a path that they haven't walked on themselves? They must have the licence (known as Ijazah in Arabic) from their Murshid to be able to guide others. Not every disciple is honoured with this role. When a spiritual master hands over the licence in Tasawwuf, it is usually done with an indication from the Prophet peace be upon him, whether it's a dream of the Prophet peace be upon him they see or spiritual visions whilst awake. As the true men of Allah (Awliyah), they have the connection to see the Prophet; peace be upon them. A genuine teacher will never show off and proclaim that they have seen the Prophet, peace be upon him, as this is a form of arrogance. If you are sincere about finding a true guide, you will feel their spiritual aura around you. You will feel more uplifted and will forget about worldly issues when in their presence. This is because they have done so much Zikr and sent so many salutations to the

Prophet, peace be upon him, throughout their lives that there is always a refreshing and spiritually uplifted presence around them. In the west, we say, "passing the torch." In Tasawwuf, this is only done when the disciple has reached a certain level of knowledge of the Shariah and has progressed more than the average person on the path of spirituality. Usually, the disciple will be free from arrogance and selfishness; they won't lie or have bad intentions in their hearts or greed. This is why, in true Sufism, it is up to the Prophet, peace be upon him, to make the final decision about whether they should be honoured to have the torch passed down to them. As he peace be upon him, he is aware of the state of the spiritual disciples. If there is any doubt that the person will start abusing his licence to teach, then they won't be bestowed with it anyway. This is for pure authentic spiritual chains (silsila's). Another sign that the spiritual guide is upright will be in his followers. His followers will be religiously educated and will have good manners. All of the fake Sufi's I have seen in my experiences have followers who are uneducated to the extent that they can't even recite the Quran.

Once the guide, Shaykh, or Murshid has met these major criteria, if one is comfortable, they may give their allegiance to them. This is an action that the companions took with the Prophet, peace be upon him. It's more of a promise that you will obey them and follow their path. A true guide will only advise good. By obeying them. You will eventually get closer to Allah and his Prophet, peace be upon him. This allegiance is known as "Bayah or Bayat." There is evidence of this in the Quran and Sunnah.

$$\text{لَّقَدْ رَضِيَ ٱللَّهُ عَنِ ٱلْمُؤْمِنِينَ إِذْ يُبَايِعُونَكَ تَحْتَ ٱلشَّجَرَةِ فَعَلِمَ مَا فِي قُلُوبِهِمْ فَأَنزَلَ ٱلسَّكِينَةَ عَلَيْهِمْ وَأَثَـٰبَهُمْ فَتْحًا قَرِيبًا}$$

Translation: Indeed, Allah was pleased with the believers when they pledged allegiance to you ˹O Prophet˺ under the tree. He knew what was in their hearts, so He sent down serenity upon them and rewarded them with a victory at hand, (Surah Al-Fath, Verse 18)

'Ubadah ibn al-Samit reported: We pledged allegiance to the Messenger of Allah, peace and blessings be upon him, on the condition that we would listen to and obey our leaders, in adversity and in prosperity, in what we favour and in what we dislike, even if he commits favouritism against us, and that we would not dispute with those in authority unless definitive unbelief is seen from them for which there is clear proof from Allah Almighty, and that we would speak the truth in every circumstance without fearing the rebuke of anyone. (Ṣaḥīḥ al-Bukhārī 7055, Ṣaḥīḥ Muslim 1709)

You are only allowed to have one spiritual guide. It is like studying for an exam at numerous institutes. Although the aim is to pass the exam for the same subject at the same level of education, For example, you're in your 3rd and final year at university studying math. If someone starts taking knowledge from numerous institutes and tutors, the student will become more confused as the exam date gets closer. The various teaching methods and differences in the syllabus will have a catastrophic effect on the student, and more damage than good will occur. This is the same as spirituality; you are only allowed one spiritual guide (Murshid). Unless, before they pass away, they tell you to obey one of his successors, then that's normal practice. Because you will still be under the same teachings and the same syllabus (meaning the same chain/Silsila). Just because the spiritual guide passes away doesn't mean your spiritual improvement stops. You still do what the Shaykh has prescribed you to do. This is why it is crucial to carry out deep research on the chain (Silsila) and the spiritual guide before giving your oath of allegiance to them. Unless you discover that the guide is fraudulent, then the Bayah (allegiance) is not intact, as he's a fake guide anyway.

The most prominent Sufi chains (Silsila) are Naqshbandi, Chistiyyah, Qadriayah, Mujaddadiyah, Soharwadiyah, and Shadhili. These are most popular as the predecessors of these chains spread their teaching methods around the world. In total, there are around 41 Sufi chains, as mentioned earlier. The reason for adding this chapter is to give the reader an understanding that spiritual paths do exist and one has the ability to reach higher spiritual states if they wish, which should be the goal of all Muslims. Your character will improve significantly, and you will develop as a person. This will give you a better understanding of the religion as you become more conscious of Allah, regardless of your surroundings.

These are a list of classical Sufi shaykhs whose numerous books you can read to get a better understanding of Sufism.

These are a list of classical Sufi shaykhs whose numerous books you can read to get a better understanding of Sufism.

Shaykh Abdul Qadir Jilani
Imam Ghazali
Shaykh Muhee-Udeen Ibn Arabi
Imam Jalal-Udeen As-Suyuti
Shah Wali-Ullah Muhaddith Dhelwi
Mawlana Jalal-Udeen Rumi
Shaykh Ali Hujweri

Below is a list of great Sufi Shaykhs who have authored contemporary books which you will find beneficial.:
Shaykh Nazim Al-Haqqani
Shaykh Habib Umar Bin Hafiz
Shaykh Muhammad Al-Yacoubi
Shaykh Habib Ali Jifri
Shyakh Nuh Ha Mim Keller
Shaykh Martin Lings

There are numerous more. However, I have included enough contemporary Sufi Shaykhs whose works are more than beneficial. Towards the end of this chapter, I will provide a further reading list.

Everything I have written in this chapter is from my experience and can be found in books by the authors named above. On the other hand, with my own personal experiences of being connected to a Sufi chain, I can say that it was one of the best decisions I made. I am grateful that Allah has guided me to a true Shaykh of the spiritual path. I have developed as a person and have started to see things from various perspectives as I grew older and with the help of my teacher. This is something I strongly recommend to those interested in Islam or wanting to be a Muslim or a better Muslim. Do not let so-called religious people divert you from this path. If there's no spiritual improvement, then what have you accomplished in life? You have just lived a physical life without experiencing the path of how one can get to know God through the paths that those he loves have walked.

The importance of Tasawwuf has been made clear by the Imams of the four schools of thought, as they themselves were followers of Sufism. Below are statements on the essence of spirituality by the four imams themselves.

Imam Abu Hanifah

"If it were not for two years, I would have perished." He said, "For two years I accompanied Imam Ja'far as-Sadiq and I acquired the spiritual knowledge that made me a gnostic in the way." (Ad-Durr al-Mukhtar, vol 1. p.43)

Imam Maalik

"Whoever studies Jurisprudence (Fiqh) and didn't study Sufism [Tasawwuf] will be corrupted; and whoever studied Sufism and didn't study Jurisprudence will become a heretic; and whoever combined both will reach the truth." ('Ali al-Adawi, vol. 2, p 195)

Imam Shafi

"I accompanied the Sufi people and I received from them three knowledge's: how to speak; how to treat people with leniency and a soft heart... and they guided me in the ways of Sufism." (Kashf al-Khafa, 'Ajluni, vol. 1, p 341)

Imam Ahmad Bin Hanbal

"O my son, you have to sit with the People of Sufism, because they are like a fountain of knowledge and they keep the Remembrance of Allah in their hearts. They are the ascetics and they have the most spiritual power." (Tanwir al-Qulub p. 405)

Here are some sayings of famous classical Islamic scholars which are accepted by numerous Islamic sects:

Imam Al-Ghazali

"I knew verily that Sufis are the seekers in Allah's Way, and their conduct is the best conduct, and their way is the best way, and their manners are the most sanctified. They have cleaned their hearts from other than Allah and they have made them as pathways for rivers to run receiving knowledge of the Divine Presence." (Al-Munqidh, p. 131)

Fakhr Ad-Deen Ar-Raazi

"The way of Sufis for seeking Knowledge is to disconnect themselves from this worldly life, and they keep themselves constantly busy with Dhikrullah (remembrance of Allah), in all their actions and behaviours." (Itiqadaat Furaq al-Muslimeen, p. 72-73)

Imam Nawawi

"The specifications of the way of the Sufis are to keep the Presence of Allah in your heart in public and in private; to follow the Sunnah of the Prophet (s), and to be happy with what Allah gave you." (Maqasid at-tawhid), p. 201

Jalaluddin As-Suyuti

"As Tasawwuf in itself is the best and most honourable knowledge. It explains how to follow the Sunnah of the Prophet (s) and to put aside innovation."(Tayid Al-Haqiqat Al-Aiiyya, p. 57)

To keep this book short, I will be ending this chapter here. I hope from this chapter the reader can understand the importance of practising spirituality and how Islam is not just limited to praying 5 times a day. You can find endless books on Sufism, and I may publish one in the near future. Below I have given a reading list for those who wish to read further into Islamic spirituality.

To keep this book short, I will be ending this chapter here. I hope from this chapter the reader can understand the importance of practicing spirituality and how Islam is not just limited to praying five times a day. You can find endless books on Sufism, and I may publish one in the near future. Below, I have given a reading list for those who wish to read further into Islamic spirituality.

Further reading list on Sufism

- The secret of secrets – By Hazrat Abdul Qadir Jilani
- Akhbar Al-Akhyar – By Shah Abdul Haqq Muhaddith Dhelwi
- Sea without shore – By Shaykh Nuh Ha Mim Keller
- Ihya Ulum Uddeen – Imam Ghazali (This is an encyclopaedia of scholarly level, in recent years chapters of this book have been published in English which is better for the audience of this book)

- Ihya Ulum Uddeen: Book 22 & book 23: Discipling the soul & breaking of the two desires (translated by T.J.Winter)
- Mercy oceans – By Shaykh Nazim Al-Haqqani
- The Sufi science of self-realisation – By Shaykh Hisham Kabbani
- Sufism: its essence and the traits of its people – By Shaykh Habib Umar Bin Hafiz
- What is Sufism? – By Martin Lings

Chapter 13

The end of times, resurrection & the day of Judgment

Signs of the day of judgement

The Prophet, peace be upon him, gave us many indications as to when the day of judgement will be close. Many of these signs have already happened. Such as the physical passing of the Prophet, peace be upon him. The splitting of the moon, which the Prophet peace be upon him did. Imposters claim to be prophets. These are some of the signs of judgement that have already happened. Even though they happened centuries ago. Today, we see a lot of signs of judgement taking place within our society. Such as the widespread use of fornication and the consumption of alcohol. The increase in earthquakes. Time will lose its blessing and go by rapidly. The increase in bloodshed is something we are seeing more and more. The number of wealthy people will increase. This is something that is ongoing. With the modern age of technology, more people are finding new ways to gain wealth. A time will come when it will be difficult to find someone who is eligible for Zakaat. This is obviously still a long way to go. But we can see the signs happening right before us. Over the last few decades, we have seen prominent Islamic scholars pass away. This is also a sign of the end of times, as this is how Allah removes knowledge from the masses by taking away pure Islamic scholars who were firm in Islam and in their faith. These are the true scholars who held the light of the Prophet; peace be upon them. Their knowledge and wisdom will be eradicated, leading to more destruction for humankind. Another sign of the day of judgement is that even though women are clothed, they will be naked. Unfortunately, we see this even with so-called religious clothing, where the figure of the person can be seen explicitly. One sign indicating the end of times that we have seen in recent years that the Prophet peace be upon him warned us of is that the river Euphrates will dry up and reveal a mountain of gold. When the mountain of gold gets revealed, for every 100 people going there to take the gold, 99 people will die due to bloodshed. So far, we have seen the river dry up; only Allah knows how long it will be until the gold is revealed. People will tend to neglect the Sunnah of the Prophet, peace be upon him. Unfortunately, we can see this amongst Muslims nowadays who will skip out on his practices.

A sign towards the end of time is that the Prophet, peace be upon him, stated that for every man, there will be 50 women. This is the ratio of how outnumbered men will be compared to women. This hadith is narrated in the collection of Ibn Majaah. Another hadith stated in Ibn Majah, the Prophet peace be upon him, informed us that knowledge will be taken away (via the passing of true scholars), ignorance will prevail, and there will be much killing. Trust amongst people will also depart from the hearts of humans. In these times and ages, due to the greed of the world, many people are breaking trust for their own benefit. A hadith narrated by Abu Hurairah, complied by Imam Bukhari, states that the Prophet peace be upon him said that the hour will not come until a man passes by the grave of another man and says, "Would that I were in his place?" This obviously isn't just for men. People in general will envy those who have passed away. These thoughts will arise amongst people due to the hardships they will face in one's life as part of the trials and tribulations that we all will face. As Muslims, we believe in the next life, and we will be so fed up with this life due to our problems that we will wish to be among those who have passed. Muslims should not want death, as this is against the Sunnah (practice) of the Prophet, peace be upon him. This is why unity, love, and community cohesion are important in our societies, regardless of faith or colour. When someone is in need, we should try to help them. More importantly, the one being helped shouldn't take advantage of others by always asking for help and by not breaking trust. This is the problem we see today. Because people have abused receiving help from others, not many people want to help, even if they're in the position to do so.

A good Muslim will always keep their word. If, for example, you borrow money from someone, you should give them the timeframe you expect to pay it back. This is what the Prophet, peace be upon him, taught us. In my experience, the more practices of the Prophet, peace be upon him, we adopt, the happier these people tend to be. They have more of a positive aura around them. This leads on to the Sunnah of always trying to think optimistically, as the Prophet, peace be upon him, always thought positively even after all the struggles he went through in his life. Not only that, peace be upon him, but he was also aware of what would happen to people and circumstances around the world after his passing. With the knowledge he had and how he was always hopeful, thinking positively is a miracle. The Prophet, peace be upon him, stated that on Monday's and Thursday's, the deeds of his nation are sent to him, and if he sees people amongst his nation in error, he prays for them to Allah for forgiveness, and when he sees good, he praises Allah (Compilation of Imam Tirmizi). With all our sins being shown to him, imagine how upset he must be with us. But he doesn't give up on us; he remains hopeful, so we may change for the better. There are few narrations of the Prophet peace be upon stating that those who do not deserve a position of authority will become leaders and that this is a sign of the nearness of the day of judgement. People who are truthful will be disbelieved, and people will believe the lairs towards the end of time. Those who are genuinely trustworthy will be deemed untrustworthy, while those who are evil will be deemed trustworthy.

When the hour of final existence occurs, there will be no believers on earth. People with pure faith will have passed away by then, as Allah does not want the punishment of the hour to descend upon those who believe in him, and the Prophet peace be upon him as the final messenger. When the hour of the end of the world comes, the most evil people will be in existence.

Imam Mahdi

As the days of judgement get closer, Imam Mahdi will appear. He will be born into the lineage of the Prophet, peace be upon him, through Hazrat Fatima. According to the narrations of the Prophet, peace be upon him, Imam Mahdi will rule for 7 years and bring justice to the world. By the time Imam Mahdi appears, Dajjal will have already come into the earth and caused more oppression in the world. Imam Mahdi will liberate Jerusalem for the last time. He will also go to Syria to battle with the army of Dajjal (the anti-Christ). When Imam Mahdi arrives, he will easily be recognised by the believers. They will then pledge allegiance to him, as he will be the ruler of the entire Muslim nation.

Dajjal (the anti-christ)

Only after the appearance of Imam Mahdi will the anti-Christ (Dajjal) emerge. He will cause severe destruction in the world, similar to what we see now. Where oppression is being carried out on innocent people around the globe, The Prophet, peace be upon him, states that he will be one-eyed and will have the word"kaafir" (disbeliever) written between his eyes in Arabic. The Prophet, peace be upon him, gave us a remedy to protect ourselves from the anti-Christ. This is to memorise and recite the first 10 verses of Surah Al-Khaf (The Cave, chapter 18 of the Quran). Although the Dajjal (Anti-Christ) will have immense power, he will not have the ability to enter Makkah or Madinah. As the Prophet, peace be upon him, stated, neither plagues nor the anti-Christ will be able to affect nor enter Madinah. This narration is in the compilation of Imam Bukhari and Imam Muslim. The trials and tribulations (fitna) that will happen because of the Dajjal will be the biggest trials and tribulations people will face, as stated by the Prophet, peace be upon him, that Hadith was compiled by Imam Ahmed Bin Hanbal.

Prophet Isa (Jesus) peace be upon him

As Muslims, we believe that Prophet Isa (Jesus) was not killed. He was raised to the heavens and will descend again towards the end of time. The person they captured thinking was Jesus, peace be upon him, was another man in the same form as Jesus, as Allah says in chapter 4 of the Quran (Surah An-Nisa, chapter of the women) in verses 157–158:

$$\text{وَقَوْلِهِمْ إِنَّا قَتَلْنَا الْمَسِيحَ عِيسَى ابْنَ مَرْيَمَ رَسُولَ اللّهِ وَمَا قَتَلُوهُ وَمَا صَلَبُوهُ وَلَكِن شُبِّهَ لَهُمْ وَإِنَّ الَّذِينَ اخْتَلَفُواْ فِيهِ لَفِي شَكٍّ مِّنْهُ مَا لَهُم بِهِ مِنْ عِلْمٍ إِلاَّ اتِّبَاعَ الظَّنِّ وَمَا قَتَلُوهُ يَقِينًا بَل رَّفَعَهُ اللّهُ إِلَيْهِ وَكَانَ اللّهُ عَزِيزًا حَكِيمًا}$$

Translation: "They said, 'We have killed the Messiah, Esa the son of Maryam, the Messenger of Allah.' But they did not slay him, nor did they crucify him. Instead, a look-alike was created for them. Those who disagree about it are in doubt; they only follow assumptions. They know nothing of it except conjecture, and they certainly did not kill him. In fact, Allah raised him towards Himself; and Allah is Almighty, Wise."" (Translation of Imam Ahmed Raza Khan)

Prophet Jesus (Isa), peace be upon him, will be sent again to the world. Not as a prophet but as a follower of the nation of Prophet Muhammad, peace be upon him. Every prophet had a dua (supplication) that was accepted. For Prophet Isa (Jesus), he wished to be among the nation of the Prophet Muhammad, peace be upon him, as this is the best of all nations. As Allah answers this prayer, he will descend from the heavens back to earth to kill the Dajjal (anti-Christ). From prophetic traditions, we know that Prophet Isa (Jesus), peace be upon him, will descend during the morning prayer (Fajr). He will descend into Syria at the Ummayad

Mosque. According to a hadith collected by Imam Muslim, Prophet Isa (Jesus) will descend with his hands on the wings of two angels; his clothes will be lightly dyed with saffron; when he lowers his head, sweat beads will fall from him; and when he raises his blessed head, beads like pearls will scatter from him. At this mosque, there is a minaret called "the minaret of Isa (Jesus)." He will reach that minaret by that minaret, hence its name. That Masjid wasn't even built during the time of the Prophet, peace be upon him, yet the Prophet, peace be upon him, indicated that this is where he will descend. This goes to show the knowledge of the Prophet, peace be upon him, of future events. Prophet Isa (Jesus) will then pray behind Imam Mahdi. Prophet Isa (Jesus), peace be upon him, will capture the anti-Christ (Dajjal) in a village close to Jerusalem, and the Dajjal will be killed by what is known as the doors of Lud.

Gog (Yajuj) & Magog (Majuj)

After Prophet Isa (Jesus) kills the Dajjal (anti-Chrsit), Gog (Yajuj) and Magog (Majuj) will appear. Some people think they are two people, but they are actually two tribes. No one exactly knows where they descend from. They were captured by King Zul-Qarnayn. The story of King Zul-Qarnain and Gog (Majuj) and Magog (Majuj) can be found throughout Surah Al-Kahf (The Cave), Chapter 18 of the Quran. He was a just king who believed in Allah. He travelled around the world from west to east, as mentioned in the Quran, in Surah Al-Kahf. Until he came across two mountains, and in between them, he saw Gog (Yajuj) and Magog (Majuj), who were causing utter disruption in their society. The civilised people of that area requested King Zul-Qarnayn to build a barrier between Gog (Yajuj) and Magog (Majuj). They offered to even pay him to do this, but he refused their money as he was a king and had an abundance of wealth. However, he did request that the community, which was considered "good people," provide the King with manpower and materials to build the barrier between them. The Quran states that the use of iron, brass, and copper was requested by King Zul-Qarnain to build a dam that would hold Gog (Yajuj) and Magog (Majuj) captive. There is little information regarding the period of time during which this incident occurred. But what we do know is that the Gog (Yajuj) and Magog (Majuj) are trying to escape the dam every day. As the Prophet, peace be upon him, stated.

عَنْ أَبِي هُرَيْرَةَ، قَالَ قَالَ رَسُولُ اللَّهِ .
صلى الله عليه وسلم . " إِنَّ يَأْجُوجَ وَمَأْجُوجَ
يَحْفِرُونَ كُلَّ يَوْمٍ حَتَّى إِذَا كَادُوا يَرَوْنَ شُعَاعَ
الشَّمْسِ قَالَ الَّذِي عَلَيْهِمُ ارْجِعُوا
فَسَنَحْفِرُهُ غَدًا . فَيُعِيدُهُ اللَّهُ أَشَدَّ مَا كَانَ
حَتَّى إِذَا بَلَغَتْ مُدَّتُهُمْ وَأَرَادَ اللَّهُ أَنْ يَبْعَثَهُمْ
عَلَى النَّاسِ حَفَرُوا حَتَّى إِذَا كَادُوا يَرَوْنَ شُعَاعَ
الشَّمْسِ قَالَ الَّذِي عَلَيْهِمُ ارْجِعُوا
فَسَتَحْفِرُونَهُ غَدًا إِنْ شَاءَ اللَّهُ تَعَالَى وَاسْتَثْنَوْا
فَيَعُودُونَ إِلَيْهِ وَهُوَ كَهَيْئَتِهِ حِينَ تَرَكُوهُ
فَيَحْفِرُونَهُ وَيَخْرُجُونَ عَلَى النَّاسِ
فَيَنْشِفُونَ الْمَاءَ وَيَتَحَصَّنُ النَّاسُ مِنْهُمْ فِي
حُصُونِهِمْ فَيَرْمُونَ بِسِهَامِهِمْ إِلَى السَّمَاءِ
فَتَرْجِعُ عَلَيْهَا الدَّمُ الَّذِي اجْفَظَّ فَيَقُولُونَ
قَهَرْنَا أَهْلَ الْأَرْضِ وَعَلَوْنَا أَهْلَ السَّمَاءِ فَيَبْعَثُ
اللَّهُ نَغَفًا فِي أَقْفَائِهِمْ فَيَقْتُلُهُمْ بِهَا . قَالَ
رَسُولُ اللَّهِ . صلى الله عليه وسلم .
وَالَّذِي نَفْسِي بِيَدِهِ إِنَّ دَوَابَّ الْأَرْضِ
لَتَسْمَنُ وَتَشْكُرُ شُكْرًا مِنْ لُحُومِهِمْ .

Translation:

It was narrated from Abu Hurairah that the Messenger of Allah (ﷺ) said:

"Gog and Magog people dig every day until, when they can almost see the rays of the sun, the one in charge of them says: "Go back and we will dig it tomorrow." Then Allah puts it back, stronger than it was before. (This will continue) until, when their time has come, and Allah wants to send them against the people, they will dig until they can almost see the rays of the sun, then the one who is in charge of them will say: "Go back, and we will dig it tomorrow if Allah wills.' So they will say: "If Allah wills." Then they will come back to it and it will be as they left it. So they will dig and will come out to the people, and they will drink all the water. The people will fortify themselves against them in their fortresses. They will shoot their arrows towards the sky and they will come back with blood on them, and they will say: "We have defeated the people of earth and dominated the people of heaven." Then Allah will send a worm in the napes of their necks and will kill them thereby.'" The Messenger of Allah (ﷺ) said: "By the One in Whose Hand is my soul, the beasts of the earth will grow fat on their flesh."

The above hadith is found in the compilation of Ibn Majah. We can see from this hadith that every day they try to break out of the dam, but when they rest, Allah bounds them back in the dam. When they manage to release themselves, that's when the hour of judgement is very close. When they release themselves, they will come out in mass numbers and drink from the lake of Tiberias in Palestine until it is dry. All of this will only occur once Prophet Isa (Jesus), peace be upon him, has killed the Dajjal (anti-Christ). When Gog (Yajuj) and Magog (Majuj) arrive, Prophet Isa (Jesus), peace be upon him, and the believers on earth will take refuge in Mount Tur (the mountain of olives) in Palestine, until Allah kills off Gog and Magog as stated in the above Hadith. Once they have been killed, Allah will order for the rain to pour until their bodies have been swept into the sea and to remove the foul smell on earth of their corpses.

Currently, in Madinah, next to the Prophet's tomb, there is an empty area within the chambers. This is the place that Prophet Jesus (Isa), peace be upon him, will be buried, as when he does descend from the heavens, once his missions are complete, he will pass away and be buried beside the Prophet Muhammad, peace be upon him.

The Resurrection

Regarding the resurrection, Allah has stated this throughout the Quran. Below, I have given a few verses that mention the process of the resurrection. In chapter 36 of the Quran, Surah Ya-Seen, also known as the heart of the Quran, Allah says in verses 51–54 the following:

وَنُفِخَ فِي الصُّوْرِ فَاِذَا هُمْ مِّنَ الْاَجْدَاثِ اِلٰى رَبِّهِمْ يَنْسِلُوْنَ ٥١.

"And the Trumpet will be blown - so they will come forth from the graves, running towards their Lord."

قَالُوْا يٰوَيْلَنَا مَنْ بَعَثَنَا مِنْ مَّرْقَدِنَا هٰذَا مَا وَعَدَ الرَّحْمٰنُ وَصَدَقَ الْمُرْسَلُوْنَ ٥٢.

"Saying, 'O our misfortune! Who has raised us from our sleep? This is what the Most Gracious had promised, and the Noble Messengers had spoken the truth!'"

اِنْ كَانَتْ اِلَّا صَيْحَةً وَّاحِدَةً فَاِذَا هُمْ جَمِيْعٌ لَّدَيْنَا مُحْضَرُوْنَ ٥٣.

"It is just one scream, and every one of them will be brought together before Us!"

فَالْيَوْمَ لَا تُظْلَمُ نَفْسٌ شَيْئًا وَّلَا تُجْزَوْنَ اِلَّا مَا كُنْتُمْ تَعْمَلُوْنَ ٥٤.

"So this day no soul will be wronged in the least; and you will not be compensated except for your deeds."

Allah states in the 39th chapter, Surah Az-Zumar (The Troops or The Throngs) in verse 68-70.

وَنُفِخَ فِى الصُّوَرِ فَصَعِقَ مَنْ فِى السَّمٰوٰتِ وَمَنْ فِى الْاَرْضِ اِلَّا مَنْ شَآءَ اللهُ ۚ ثُمَّ نُفِخَ فِيْهِ اُخْرٰى فَاِذَا هُمْ قِيَامٌ يَّنْظُرُوْنَ. 68

"And the Trumpet will be blown, so everyone in the heavens and everyone in the earth will fall unconscious, except whomever Allah wills; it will then be blown again, thereupon they will get up staring!"

وَاَشْرَقَتِ الْاَرْضُ بِنُوْرِ رَبِّهَا وَوُضِعَ الْكِتٰبُ وَجِآىْءَ بِالنَّبِيّٖنَ 69.وَالشُّهَدَآءِ وَقُضِىَ بَيْنَهُمْ بِالْحَقِّ وَهُمْ لَا يُظْلَمُوْن

"And the earth will shine bright by the light of its Lord, and the Book will be established, and the Prophets and this Noble Prophet and the witnesses upon them from this nation will be brought, and it will be judged between them with the truth, and they will not be wronged."

70. وَوُفِّيَتْ كُلُّ نَفْسٍ مَّا عَمِلَتْ وَهُوَ اَعْلَمُ بِمَا يَفْعَلُوْنَ

"And every soul will be repaid for its deeds in full, and He knows very well what they used to do."

Allah further states in the 78th chapter of the Quran, Surah An-Naba (The News/The Tidings) in verses 18-20

١٨. يَّوْمَ يُنْفَخُ فِي الصُّوَرِ فَتَأْتُوْنَ اَفْوَاجًا

"The day when the Trumpet will be blown – you will therefore come forth in multitudes."

١٩. وَّفُتِحَتِ السَّمَآءُ فَكَانَتْ اَبْوَابًا

"And the heaven will be opened - it therefore becomes like gates."

٢٠. وَّ سُيِّرَتِ الْجِبَالُ فَكَانَتْ سَرَابًا

"And the mountains will be moved - they will therefore become like mirages."

From the above verses, we can see the description of how the resurrection will occur. Once we pass away, we will be in our graves until then. Once we have been resurrected, the day of judgement will start. People will have to answer to Allah for all they did during their time on earth.

Judgement day

When judgement day begins, people will be bare-clothed. Due to the fear and intensity of that day, no one will look at each other lustfully. Parents will forget and not care about their own children, and vice versa.

فَإِذَا نُفِخَ فِي ٱلصُّورِ فَلَآ أَنسَابَ بَيْنَهُمْ يَوْمَئِذٍ وَلَا يَتَسَآءَلُونَ

"Then when the trumpet shall be blown there shall be no relationship among them, nor will they ask after one another".
(Surah Al-Muminoon – The Believers, Chapter 23 : Verse 101)

The entire human creation will run to every prophet, begging for help. Only for them to be turned away. Every prophet will tell the people to go to another prophet. People will first go to Prophet Adam, peace be upon him, as he's the father of humankind. He will not give them aid as he will feel guilty for disobeying Allah as he ate from the forbidden tree. He will be shy to ask Allah for help, as he believes he's in error himself. Eventually, after going from prophet to prophet, Humanity will be at the doorstep of the Prophet Muhammad; peace be upon him. He, peace be upon him, will be the only one who can help on that day. He will then go into Sujood (prostration), and he will glorify Allah and his own ways. We need to understand the love between the Prophet Muhammad (peace be upon him) and Allah. In human nature, when we love someone, whether it's friends, parents, children, or spouse, we may call them by special names to show our affection for them. Imagine the ways the Prophet, peace be upon him, calls on Allah through unique names that may not be known to us. Think about how Allah honours the Prophet, peace be upon him, and what beautiful names he calls his Prophet, through attributes that we also do not know about. Allah will then say to the Prophet, peace be upon him, to raise his head and speak to his Lord, and that he will hear what he, peace be upon him, has to say. One by one, Allah will take the entire human race to his court and question everything they have done. Whether it's a sin or taking the rights away from someone, Allah will honour humankind by keeping their sins secret and not exposing them to others. Then Allah will decide if they should be forgiven or not.

On the day of judgement, the sun will be one mile away from our heads; some will sweat up to their ankles, others to their knees, others to their waists, and some will drown in their own sweat, depending on their sins. There will be no shade that day except the shade of Allah, and he will keep those he wishes under that shade. The Prophet, peace be upon him, said:

Abu Huraira reported: The Prophet, peace and blessings be upon him, said, *"There are seven whom Allah will shade on a day when there is no shade but His. They are a just ruler, a youth who grew up in the worship of Allah, one whose heart is attached to the mosques, two who love each other, meet each other, and depart from each other for the sake of Allah, a man who is tempted by a beautiful woman of high status but he rejects her (refraining from fornication when one has an easy chance to commit it), saying, 'I fear Allah,' and one who spends in charity and hides it such that his right hand does not know what his left hand has given, and one who remembered Allah in private and he wept."* (Bukhari and Muslim).

The fortunate people will drink from the pond of Kawthar. That drink will cleanse them of their sins, so they may enter paradise in a pure state. We will all be required to cross the bridge above the hellfire. Known as "Siraat". The bridge will be thinner than a strand of hair and sharper than a knife. According to some, the bridge will take around 1,500 years to cross. However, those pious will cross it quicker than a blink of an eye. Those who were not that practicing may find themselves in trouble. I hope the readers of this book can understand the difficulty the day of judgement will have on us. This is why I included the chapter on spiritual refinement and following a spiritual guide. To clean oneself of errors in the hope that the next life may be lighter for us than expected. But only if God wills. All we can do is try our best and leave the rest to Allah. Tonnes of books can be written on the process of judgement day alone. I will keep this brief and may add more on this subject in the 2nd edition of this book. Although there is a lot to fear, Muslims should remain hopeful and do the best they can while on this earth.

Chapter 14

General Questions & Answers

This section of the book will cover general questions and answers that new Muslims or those interested in Islam tend to ask, based on my experiences.

1. Do Muslims have to pray five times a day?

Yes, they should try to pray at the prescribed time. Although this may seem like a basic question, Unfortunately, some new Muslims may feel the need to ask this as they have seen some of their Muslim friends not praying on a daily basis.

2. If my family does not support my decision to be a Muslim, What should I do?

To avoid conflict, one should discuss the matter with the family as to why they oppose one converting to Islam. Usually, it's due to a lack of knowledge. Once the concerns arise, you will be able to put your argument forward in an amicable manner. If this doesn't work, you may find it useful to bring in external family members, friends, or anyone else you see fit in the community to try to address your family. At the end of the day, if you sincerely believe that Islam is the religion of truth, Then you should not let your family or anyone else put you off. At the end of the day, each one of us will die alone and be buried in our own graves. If they keep refusing to support you, you should not be deterred from practicing your faith. Whether you wish to declare it to everyone or not is up to you. Only you are aware of your situation. However, when accepting Islam and testifying that you believe Allah is one and that the Prophet, peace be upon him, is the final messenger, you should have witnesses around you. One of the reasons is that if you die, then you should have a funeral according to the Islamic method. If witnesses are present, then during this time they will be able to notify your family that you are indeed a Muslim. There have been occasions where people have been kicked out of the house for accepting Islam as their faith. Remember the life of the Prophet; peace be upon him, his family, and his companions. Many practiced Islam in secrecy at first. This is more difficult for women, as covering the body may be challenging. Women in this situation should remember that Allah is all-knowing and all-forgiving. Every Muslim has their own test in this world, and this may be yours. There are other options. Such as moving out of the family house, if you have the confidence, but you should weigh the pros and cons of this. You may love your family and not feel comfortable living away from them. As this is a huge dilemma, one should seek religious guidance from a local Sunni imam. Everyone's issues can be complex in their own different ways. There is no right answer for everyone.

You may have to pray in secrecy if it's away from home. It could be the local mosque where you work, prayer rooms in shopping malls and hospitals, university campuses, etc. This situation is slightly easier for men, as a hijab (covering the hair) is not necessary for them.

This may be harder to keep concealed around family gatherings where Haraam food and alcohol may be served. In this case, it is permissible to come up with a justified reason as to why you are refraining from alcohol and Haraam food items.

3. My friends have distanced themselves from me due to my being a Muslim. What should I do?

If that's the case, then it exposes how much of a bad friend or friends they are in the first place. You should consider yourself lucky that they have distanced themselves from you. Being a new Muslim could be tough. But you should encourage yourself to find new good-practicing Muslims. This could be the make or break for any new Muslim. If you hang around with too many non-Muslim friends, their morals and practices may rub off on you. Taking away the light of faith. On the other hand, the Muslims you may choose to associate with. You should make sure of how well-practiced they are in the faith and how their character is. Just because someone prays five times a day doesn't make them a good Muslim. They may pray five times a day, tell tales, and be two-faced. What good is your worship going to be, then? Luckily, with modern-day technology, there are numerous forums and social media pages one can associate themselves with to build a network with like-minded Muslims. In most areas, the local Masjid (Mosque) should have circles for men and women that they may participate in.

4. My current job role doesn't allow me to pray on time or doesn't have prayer facilities. What should I do?

In the modern era where governments are trying to make things "equal," if your employer doesn't give you the time and space for prayer, you should raise this with them immediately. In reality, they can't say no, as that may be classified as discrimination. On the other hand, in a lot of western countries, by law, employers don't necessarily have to give you the facilities to pray. You should try to get colleagues to back you, as the more voices that are raised, the more likely some positive change will happen. If it keeps failing, the choice is yours. You seek employment elsewhere, notifying them before you start the role that, as a Muslim, you are required to pray on time (bearing in mind that prayer times change throughout the year). This should cause the conversation to be less awkward as you're raising this with them from the start. You can offer them to give you extra breaks or an extended break and communicate with them. There are stories I know of Muslims who have asked the employer to give them unpaid extra breaks or unpaid extended breaks just so they can fulfil the obligation of praying, which for a Muslim should be more important than anything.

If you are someone who can't hold their appointment for long periods of time, then this should also be mentioned to the employer that you may be gone for longer than required. This is why Muslims should try their best to practice keeping onto one's ablution (Wudu) without causing pain to their health. For example, if you need to use the bathroom more than regular, then you obviously should use it and not hold onto your ablution. As this can lead to health issues in the future. In modern times, I'm sure employers will be more than happy to accommodate. If it means you have to stay an extra hour or so after your colleagues have left, then so be it. Because prayer is the most important aspect of a Muslim's life. On a final note, Muslims in workplaces who do not raise this issue should be ashamed of themselves. It makes Muslims look like a joke and shows that they aren't serious about their faith. This also causes issues for someone who is a practicing Muslim. Because the employer can turn around and say, "Well, there are other Muslims who work here, and they don't pray or have asked for time off to pray, so why should we let you pray?" This happened to me once when I was 17 years old. I walked out of that door straight away and never looked back. I left with my head held high, standing up for my beliefs, and so should you. Maybe with a hard approach, the culture of praying at work may change.

5. I want to convert to Islam, but my spouse doesn't, nor do I want to leave him or her. What can be done?

This is a complex scenario, but something that's not new. There have been cases where a married person wants to convert but is adamant that they will not leave their partner. Some have even gone to the extent of saying they would rather remain non-Muslim if it meant they would have to leave their partner rather than convert to Islam and leave their spouse. Even though they know the religion of Islam is the truth, In this case, we need to look at the lesser of two evils. The answer also varies if it is the man who is converting. As in Islam, men are allowed to marry people of the book. Meaning Jews of Christians. Women, however, must marry a Muslim. If the husband wants to convert, and if he is married to a person of the Jewish or Christian faith, then it is permissible, and the marriage is still binding from an Islamic point of view. If the wife is an atheist or belongs to another religion, then we should consider the advantages and disadvantages. Let me ask you. Is it better to remain in a marriage and for at least one of the partners to enter Islam? They will still enter Islam and can expect paradise in the next life. Or if they are strongly pointing out that they will not sacrifice their partner and not convert to Islam? At least it is better to be a Muslim than not to be a Muslim. Usually, in these scenarios, the person will be strongly fond of Islam if these questions arise, as it shows their seriousness. By Islamic law, as marriage is not allowed of a Muslim man to any female of other religions with the exception of them being a Jew or Christian, then they will be considered living in fornication. This is the same if the wife converts and the husband doesn't want to convert. So what is better? To be a non-Muslim, or to be a Muslim and be in sin? As mentioned earlier, Allah is merciful and aware of our circumstances. Humans will easily judge a person in this situation, but Allah's methods are different. Even if you are a Muslim and living in sin, there is hope that Allah will surely forgive you if you repent. You would be surprised by how many people in this situation have had their partners convert after some time. Because they will see the positive change within you. They will see an improvement in life quality, knowledge, and character. So it is essential not to give up hope and to keep praying to Allah to open the hearts of spouses so they may also enter Islam. It is important that you remain a positive ambassador of the religion to show the beauty of Islam to your spouse and other family members. As long as one of the spouses is supportive of your decision, this will reduce a lot of conflict. At first, it can be a big jump. Your spouse may see you praying and living your life differently, but over time, these adjustments will become the norm.

6. I am a female who has recently converted. Am I allowed to travel alone?

Generally, in Islam, women are not permitted to travel alone. Especially during darkness. The word "travel" in this context is used by the Islamic definition of being a traveller (Musaafir), which one is classified as if they travel over 48 miles. This is for safety concerns. Except for absolute necessities, Muslim women should travel with their husbands or a male family.

7. What preparations can I take if I want to accept Islam?

One should not unnecessarily delay accepting Islam. Upon accepting Islam, you should start by acquiring knowledge of the tenants of faith and understanding the five pillars of Islam. Once you've grasped a fair amount of knowledge, you should focus on refining your daily activities and diet. Try to avoid Haraam food and alcohol if you are currently consuming them, and slowly prepare yourself for testifying your faith. However, it is important not to delay accepting Islam. The devil can whisper to us, known as Waas-Wasa. Satan will try to come up with many tricks to change your mind on conversion. If you think you can't wait long, then one shouldn't. You can always make changes after becoming a Muslim. But it will be important to find the right group of people to help you make these changes, as I said earlier.

8. Do you have to say "peace be upon him" when mentioning a prophet?

Yes. When mentioning any of the Prophet's names, it is recommended to say peace be upon him in any language due to respect.

9. How many prophets and scriptures do Muslims believe in?

Muslims believe that there were 124,000 prophets. However, only 25 are mentioned in the Quran. There have been 104 scriptures revealed to various prophets. 4 of these scriptures are the major books, such as the Torah (Tawraat = Arabic) revealed to Prophet Musa (Moses) peace be upon him, the Psalms (Zaboor = Arabic) revealed to Prophet Dawood (David) peace be upon him, the Gospel (Injeel = Arabic) revealed to Prophet Isa (Jesus) peace be upon him, and the Quran revealed to Prophet Muhammad peace be upon him. The other 100 books are smaller revelations, such as scrolls revealed to numerous other prophets. The prophets mentioned in the Quran are listed below:

1. Prophet Adam (peace be upon him) (mentioned 25 times in the Quran)

2. Prophet Idris (Enoch), peace be upon him (mentioned twice in the Quran).

3. Prophet Nuh (Noah), peace be upon him (mentioned 43 times in the Quran).

4. Prophet Hud (Eber), peace be upon him (mentioned seven times in the Quran)

5. Prophet Saalih (Methusaleh), peace be upon him (mentioned nine times in the Quran)

6. Prophet Lut (Lot), peace be upon him (mentioned 27 times in the Quran)

7. Prophet Ibrahim (Abrahman), peace be upon him (mentioned 69 times in the Quran)

8. Prophet Ismail (Ishmael), peace be upon him (mentioned 12 times in the Quran)

9. Prophet Ishaaq (Isaac), Peace be upon him (mentioned 17 times in the Quran)

10. Prophet Yaqub (Jacob), peace be upon him (mentioned 16 times in the Quran)

11. Prophet Yusuf (Joseph), peace be upon him (mentioned 27 times in the Quran)

12. Prophet Shuaib (Jethra), peace be upon him (mentioned 11 times in the Quran)

13. Prophet Ayyub (Job), peace be upon him (mentioned four times in the Quran)

14. Prophet Dhul-Kifl (Ezekiel), peace be upon him (mentioned twice in the Quran)

15. Prophet Musa (Moses), peace be upon him (mentioned 136 times in the Quran)

16. Prophet Harun (Aaron), peace be upon him (mentioned 20 times in the Quran)

17. Prophet Dawood (David), peace be upon him (mentioned 16 times in the Quran)

18. Prophet Sulaymaan (Solomon), peace be upon him (mentioned 17 times in the Quran)

19. Prophet Ilyaas (Elias), peace be upon him (mentioned twice in the Quran)

20. Prophet Alyasa (Elisha), peace be upon him (mentioned twice in the Quran)

21. Prophet Yunus (Jonah), peace be upon him (mentioned four times in the Quran)

22. Prophet Zakariyya (Zachariah), peace be upon him (mentioned seven times in the Quran)

23. Prophet Yahya (John the Baptist), peace be upon him (mentioned five times in the Quran)

24. Prophet Isa (Jesus), peace be upon him (mentioned 25 times in the Quran)

25. Prophet Muhammad, peace be upon him (mentioned four times in the Quran)

10. How should new Muslims prepare for Ramadan?

This can be quite difficult when you are a new Muslim. I strongly recommend taking preparations three months before the month of

Ramadan. Especially if it is your first Ramadan. You most likely never fasted before. You should prepare physically, mentally, and spiritually. You can start off by reducing the number of meals you take throughout the day. Then you can slowly decrease your water consumption. Whichever order works better for you. Then you can develop the habit of not eating or drinking for half of the day and eventually throughout the entire day. To practice the full day of fasting. You can fast on your days off if it makes it easier. You can then slowly introduce if you wish to fast on Sunnah days, such as Monday's and Thursday's. Or, what is known as the "white days" in the Islamic tradition? Which are the 13th, 14th, and 15th days of the Arabic month.

Once you have controlled your consumption of food and drink, you can then cut back and try to totally avoid other aspects of fasting, which are also important. Such as lying, gossiping, and backbiting (not that Muslims should be doing this anyway, but it's best to make a start sooner rather than later) and refraining from conjugal relations with your spouse. These acts severely decrease the rewards of fasting. Some scholars even say it's a method of breaking your fast by lying, backbiting, etc. Conjugal relations with your spouse definitely break your fast. The month of Ramadan is more than just starving yourself. That's actually the easiest aspect of fasting. Controlling one's ego and thoughts and improving behaviour and character is the bigger picture of fasting,

11. Do Muslims have to eat meat?

Muslims don't have to eat meat, but they should, as this is a Sunnah of the Prophet, peace be upon him, to eat meat, which is Halal (permissible) as long as it is slaughtered the Islamic way. This could be chicken, turkey, beef, lamb, venison, fish, camel, and even rabbit. As the Prophet, peace be upon him, ate Rabbit, according to a few narrations. Although it's permissible for Muslims to be vegetarians or vegans, in order not to resemble people of other faiths, they should occasionally add some form of red and/or white meat to their meals, even if it's once a week.

12. Is Hajj (major pilgrimage) mandatory?

Hajj is one of the pillars of Islam, and Muslims are required to perform Hajj at least once in their lives if they have the finances and health. Hajj can be physically stressful for most people due to the heat and the amount of walking that is required. One should not perform Hajj if they owe others money and/or have serious debt issues. Furthermore, Hajj is not mandatory for those who do not have an adequate health level, as you should not be burdening others with Hajj. So, if you have the money and health, you are encouraged to perform Hajj. Because you may not be in that positive financial position again, or your health may start to decline, or both.

13. How should Muslims search for a spouse?

This is more difficult for new Muslims, as they may not have a larger, wider network. First of all, one should avoid dating sites, as these cause more issues than positivity. You should aim to get your family involved and try to find someone known to the family or community. It is essential to always get the opinions of others when choosing a spouse, as this is a life decision. Usually, mosques (masjids) should have a matrimonial service that you can use. When choosing a partner, you should aim to prioritise character and level of religious practice. Although the Sunnah is to first prioritise how religiously practicing they are and how much knowledge they have, In the modern era, we have seen a change in people's behaviour. There are practicing Muslims who pray five times a day but have the most disgraceful behaviour. In these cases, you should avoid these people. It is a lot tougher to change a person's habits or character than it is to get them to practice Islam. You may be able to mould a person who possesses good manners, etc., and try to get them to practice ore. However, there is a 50/50 chance of this. In my opinion and from my experiences travelling around the world, You may see people in certain parts of the world are more practicing and have a high level of good character compared to other parts of the world. This may be something else you want to consider, as interracial marriages are allowed in Islam. Having said that, there will always be pros and cons for whoever you marry, as no one is perfect. For some odd reason, the young generation seems to find that hard to believe. This is why many Muslims learn the hard way and still remain single in their 30's or 40's because they can't find the person they've been dreaming about all their lives. This is obviously worse for women, even though some still go down this route as their chances of conceiving a child get closer to zero. Islamically, you are allowed to get to know someone before you marry them without any physical contact taking place. One shouldn't delay getting to know a person, as this widens the chances of committing sin. You should also be taking another person with you if you meet someone. This is both for men and women. Preferably a family member; this is to avoid any loose talk and get the opinion of someone else.

14. Do women have to cover their faces in Islam?

It is not mandatory for women to cover their faces. However, it is mandatory to cover your hair and the rest of your body. You can only expose your face and hands. Having said that, if you wear excessive make-up, then it defeats the purpose of dressing modestly and covering yourself. Women should not wear make-up when going out of the house, as this is not necessary. You're only inviting men to gaze at you (not that being bare-faced won't mean men won't look at you, but since you have the power to mitigate it, then you should). If you're at home with family and around men that you cannot marry (Mahram), such as brothers and uncles, then feel free to wear make-up, but should be limited as it's not necessary. However, one should still try to dress modestly.

15. What are the Islamic months?

1. Muharram

2. Safar

3. Rabi-Ul-Awwal
   (month of the Prophet, peace be upon him's birth)

4. Rabi-Uth-Thaani

5. Jamaad-Ul-Ula

6. Jamaad-Ul-Akhir

7. Rajab

8. Shabaan

9. Ramdaan (month of fasting)

10. Shawwal

11. Zil-Qadah

12. Zil-Hijjah (month of Hajj)

NOTE: The Islamic calendar goes 10 days behind every year compared to the Gregorian calendar. This is why, for example, in some years Ramadan will be different seasons (winter, summer, etc.) over the course of years due to the Islamic calendar going back. In Islamic months, there are either 29 or 30 days, depending on the sighting of the moon. Unlike the Gregorian calendar, where February can have 28 days (or 29) and other months have 31 days,.

Chapter 15

Short Surahs (chapters from the Quran)

&

Dua's (Supplications)

In this chapter, I have added short chapters from the Quran, so one may practice reciting them as well as trying to memorise them for prayer. To make it easier for the readers, I have added a transliteration to help with pronunciation. The translation has been added so one may understand what is being said in the verses below. I strongly recommend that the readers learn the proper recitation of the Quran with a qualified local Sunni teacher. To know the art of reciting the Quran, one must learn the rules regarding it. This is known as the study of "Tajweed." When learned diligently with a qualified teacher, the student will be able to understand and practice the correct pronunciation of the Arabic letters, as this can be challenging for many. Especially those from non-Arabic backgrounds. Students, when studying Tajweed, will also understand why some letters and conditions need to be read in a lengthy manner while others are not.

When starting the recitation of the Quran, one must recite

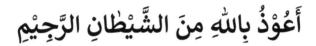

Transliteration:
A-uzu-billah-He Min-Ash-Shaytan-Nir-Rajeem

Translation:
"I seek refuge with Allah from the accursed Satan"

Once you have read this. When beginning a chapter of the Quran must recite what is known as the Basmala. Which is:

Transliteration:
Bis-mil-laa-hir Rahmaa-nir Raheem

Translation:
"In the name of Allah the most affectionate, the most merciful"

Chapter 1: Surah Al-Fatiha (The Opening)
7 Verse – 27 Words – 140 Letters

بِسْمِ اللهِ الرَّحْمٰنِ الرَّحِيْمِ ١

Transliteration:
Bis-mil-laa-hir Rahmaa-nir Raheem

Translation:
"In the name of Allah the most affectionate, the most merciful" – 1

اَلْحَمْدُ لِلّٰهِ رَبِّ الْعٰلَمِيْنَ ٢

Transliteration:
Alhamdu lillaahi Rabbil Aalameen

Translation:
"Allah praise be unto Allah, Lord of all the worlds"- 2

اَلرَّحْمٰنِ الرَّحِيْمِ ٣

Transliteration:
Ar-Rahmaa-nir-Raheem

Translation:
"The most affectionate, the merciful" – 3

مٰلِكِ يَوْمِ الدِّيْنِ ٤

Transliteration:
Maa-liki Yawm-mid-Deen

Translation:
"Master of the day of requital" – 4

اِيَّاكَ نَعْبُدُ وَاِيَّاكَ نَسْتَعِيْنُ 5

Transliteration:
Iyyaa-ka na-budu wa Iyyaa-ka nasta-een

Translation:
"We worship you alone, and beg you only for help" – 5

اِهْدِنَا الصِّرَاطَ الْمُسْتَقِيْمَ 6

Transliteration:
Ih-di-nas-siraa-tal-musta-qeem

Translation:
"Guide us on the straight path" – 6

صِرَاطَ الَّذِيْنَ اَنْعَمْتَ عَلَيْهِمْ غَيْرِ الْمَغْضُوْبِ عَلَيْهِمْ وَلَا الضَّآلِّيْنَ 7

Transliteration:
Siraa-tal-la-zeena an-amta 'alai-him
Ghay-ril-magh-dubi alahim wa-laad-daal-leen

Translation:

"The path of those whom you have favoured. Not those who have earned your anger and nor of those who have gone astray" – 7

Chapter 105: Surah Al-Feel (The Elephant)
5 Verses – 20 Words – 96 Letters

بِسْمِ اللّٰهِ الرَّحْمٰنِ الرَّحِيْمِ

Transliteration:
Bis-mil-laa-hir Rahmaa-nir Raheem

Translation:
"In the name of Allah the most affectionate, the most merciful"

اَلَمْ تَرَ كَيْفَ فَعَلَ رَبُّكَ بِاَصْحٰبِ الْفِيْلِ ١

Transliteration:
Alam-tara-kaifa-fa-ala-rab-buka-bi-as-haa-bil-feel

Translation:
"(O Beloved) Have you not seen how your Lord dealt with the companions of the elephants?" – 1

اَلَمْ يَجْعَلْ كَيْدَهُمْ فِيْ تَضْلِيْلٍ ٢

Transliteration:
Alam-yaj-al-kaida-hum-fee-tad-leel

Translation:
"Did he not cause their device to fail" – 2

وَّاَرْسَلَ عَلَيْهِمْ طَيْرًا اَبَابِيْلَ ٣

Transliteration:
Wa-ar-sala-alai-him-tai-ran-abaa-beel

Translation:
"And he sent on them swarms of birds." – 3

تَرۡمِيهِمۡ بِحِجَارَةٍ مِّنۡ سِجِّيۡلٍ ٤

Transliteration:
Tar-mee-him-bihi-jaar-ratim-min-sij-jeel

Translation:
"Striking them with stones of baked clay" – 4

فَجَعَلَهُمۡ كَعَصۡفٍ مَّأۡكُوۡلٍ ٥

Transliteration:
Faja-ala-hum-ka-as-fim-ma'-kool

Translation:
"And thus made them like broken straw, eaten up (as chaff) – 5

Chapter 106: Surah Al-Quraish (The Quraish)
4 Verses – 17 Words – 73 Letters

بِسْمِ اللهِ الرَّحْمٰنِ الرَّحِيْمِ

Transliteration:
Bis-mil-laa-hir Rahmaa-nir Raheem

Translation:
"In the name of Allah the most affectionate, the most merciful"

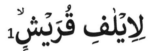

Transliteration:
Li-ee-laafi-quraish

Translation:
"Because of the attachment of the Quraish" – 1

اِلٰفِهِمْ رِحْلَةَ الشِّتَآءِ وَالصَّيْفِ ۚ

Transliteration:
Ee-laa-fi-him-rih-latash-shitaaa-i-was-saif

Translation:
"(Allah) kept them attached in their journeys during winter and summer" – 2

فَلْيَعْبُدُوْا رَبَّ هٰذَا الْبَيْتِ ۙ

Transliteration:
Fal-ya-budoo-rab-ba-haa-zal-bayt

Translation:
"So they should worship the Lord of this house (The Kabah)"
– 3

$$\text{الَّذِیْۤ اَطْعَمَهُمْ مِّنْ جُوْعٍ ۙ۬ وَّاٰمَنَهُمْ مِّنْ خَوْفٍ}$$ 4

Transliteration:
Alla-zee-ata-ama-hum-min-joo
wa-aa-mana-hum-min-khawf

Translation:
"Who has fed them against hunger and secured them from a big fear" – 4

Chapter 107: Surah Al-Ma'oon (Articles of use)
7 Verses – 25 Words – 125 Letters

بِسْمِ اللّٰهِ الرَّحْمٰنِ الرَّحِيْم

Transliteration:
Bis-mil-laa-hir Rahmaa-nir Raheem

Translation:
"In the name of Allah the most affectionate, the most merciful"

اَرَءَيْتَ الَّذِىْ يُكَذِّبُ بِالدِّيْنِ ١

Transliteration:
Ara-ay-tal-la-zee-yu-kaz-zi-bu-bid-deen

Translation:
"Well, have you seen him who belies the religion" – 1

فَذٰلِكَ الَّذِىْ يَدُعُّ الْيَتِيْمَ ٢

Transliteration:
Fa-zaa-li-ka-la-zee-ya-du-ul-ya-teem

Translation:
"That is he who drives away the orphan" – 2

وَ لَا يَحُضُّ عَلٰى طَعَامِ الْمِسْكِيْنِ ٣

Transliteration:
Wa-la-ya-hud-du-alaa-ta-aamil-mis-keen

Translation:
"And does not urge the feeding of the needy" – 3

فَوَيْلٌ لِّلْمُصَلِّينَ ٤

Transliteration:
Fa-wai-lul-lil-mus-sal-leen

Translation:
"So curse be to those offering Salaah"* – 4[3]

الَّذِينَ هُمْ عَنْ صَلَاتِهِمْ سَاهُونَ ٥

Transliteration:
Al-la-zee-na-hum-an-sa-laa-ti-him-saa-hoon

Translation:
"Who are neglectful of their Salaah" – 5

الَّذِينَ هُمْ يُرَآءُونَ ٦

Transliteration:
Al-la-zee-na-hum-yu-raa-oon

Translation:
"Those who show it (to others)" – 6

وَيَمْنَعُونَ الْمَاعُونَ ٧

---

[3] The reciter should join verse 4 and 5 together when reciting, as stopping on verse 4 has a negative meaning of the Quran.

Transliteration:
Wa-yam-na-oon-al-maa-oon

Translation:
"And refuse to give daily articles of use (to the needy ones)" – 7

Chapter 108: Surah Al-Kauthar (The Abundance of Good)
3 Verses – 10 Words – 42 Letters

بِسْمِ اللهِ الرَّحْمٰنِ الرَّحِيْمِ

Transliteration:

Bis-mil-laa-hir Rahmaa-nir Raheem

Translation:

"In the name of Allah the most affectionate, the most merciful"

اِنَّاۤ اَعْطَيْنٰكَ الْكَوْثَرَ ۱

Transliteration:

In-naa-atain-na-kal-kaw-thar

Translation:

"(O beloved Muhammad) Undoubtedly, we have bestowed upon you an abundance of good" – 1

فَصَلِّ لِرَبِّكَ وَانْحَرْ ۲

Transliteration:

Fa-sal-li-li-rab-bika-wan-har

Translation:

"So offer Salaah to your Lord and offer sacrifice" – 2

اِنَّ شَانِئَكَ هُوَ الْاَبْتَرُ ۳

Transliteration:

In-na-shaa-ni-aka-hu-wal-ab-tar

Translation:

"Verily, your enemy is deprived of every good" – 3

Chapter 109: Surah Al-Kafiroon (The Infidels)
6 Verses – 26 Words – 94 Letters

بِسْمِ اللهِ الرَّحْمٰنِ الرَّحِيْم

Transliteration:
Bis-mil-laa-hir Rahmaa-nir Raheem

Translation:
"In the name of Allah the most affectionate, the most merciful"

قُلْ يٰٓاَيُّهَا الْكٰفِرُوْنَ ₁

Transliteration:
Qul-ya-ay-yu-hal-kaa-fi-roon

Translation:
"Please declare (O beloved Muhammad) – "Oh Infidels" – 1

لَآ اَعْبُدُ مَا تَعْبُدُوْنَ ₂

Transliteration:
La-abu-du-maa-taabu-doon

Translation:
"I do not worship that which you worship" – 2

وَلَآ اَنْتُمْ عٰبِدُوْنَ مَآ اَعْبُدُ ₃

Transliteration:
Wa-la-an-tum-aabi-doona-ma-abud

239

Translation:

"Nor do you worship that whom I worship" – 3

$$\text{وَلَآ أَنَا عَابِدٌ مَّا عَبَدتُّمْ}_4$$

Transliteration:

Wa-la-ana-aabi-dhum-maa-abath-tum

Translation:

"And I shall never worship what you worship" – 4

$$\text{وَلَآ أَنْتُمْ عٰبِدُوْنَ مَآ أَعْبُدُ}_5$$

Transliteration:

Wa-la-an-tum-aabi-doona-ma-abud

Translation:

"Nor do you worship that whom I worship" – 5

$$\text{لَكُمْ دِيْنُكُمْ وَلِيَ دِيْنِ}_6$$

Transliteration:

La-kum-dee-nu-kum-wa-liya-deen

Translation:

"(Therefore) to you your religion and for me my religion" – 6

Chapter 110: Surah An-Nasr (The Help)
3 Verses – 17 Words – 77 Letters

بِسْمِ اللهِ الرَّحْمٰنِ الرَّحِيْمِ

Transliteration:
Bis-mil-laa-hir Rahmaa-nir Raheem

Translation:
"In the name of Allah the most affectionate, the most merciful"

اِذَا جَاۤءَ نَصْرُ اللهِ وَالْفَتْحُ ١

Transliteration:
Iza-jaa-a-nas-rul-laa-hi-wal-fath

Translation:
"When the help of Allah and victory comes" – 1

وَرَاَيْتَ النَّاسَ يَدْخُلُوْنَ فِىْ دِيْنِ اللهِ اَفْوَاجًا ٢

Transliteration:
Wa-ra-ay-tan-naa-sa-yad-khu-loona
Fee-dee-nil-laa-hi-af-wa-jaa

Translation:
"And you see people entering the religion of Allah in troops"
– 2

فَسَبِّحْ بِحَمْدِ رَبِّكَ وَاسْتَغْفِرْهُ،
إِنَّهُ كَانَ تَوَّابًا 3

Transliteration:
Fa-sab-bih-bi-ham-di-rab-bika-was-tagh-firh
Inna-hoo-kaa-na-taw-waa-ba

Translation:
"Then celebrate the praise of your Lord and seek his forgiveness. Surely he is most relenting" – 3

Chapter 111: Surah Al-Lahab (The Flame) (Also known as – Surah Al-Masad – Twisted Strands / The Palm Fibre) 5 Verses – 20 Words – 70 Letters

بِسْمِ اللهِ الرَّحْمٰنِ الرَّحِيْمِ

Transliteration:
Bis-mil-laa-hir Rahmaa-nir Raheem

Translation:
"In the name of Allah the most affectionate, the most merciful"

تَبَّتْ يَدَآ اَبِىْ لَهَبٍ وَّتَبَّ ۱

Transliteration:
Tab-bath-ya-daa-abee-la-ha-buyw-wa-tab

Translation:
"The hands of Abu Lahab (the father of the flame) have perished, and he too has perished" – 1

مَآ اَغْنٰى عَنْهُ مَالُهٗ وَمَا كَسَبَّ ۲

Transliteration:
Ma-agh-naa-anhu-maa-luhoo-wa-ma-ka-sab

Translation:
"His wealth and what he earned did not profit him" – 2

سَيَصْلَىٰ نَارًا ذَاتَ لَهَبٍ 3

Transliteration:
Sa-yas-la-naa-ran-zaa-ta-lahab

Translation:
"Soon shall he enter into a blazing fire" – 3

وَّامْرَاَتُهُ ۖ حَمَّالَةَ الْحَطَبِ 4

Transliteration:
Wam-ra-atu-hu-ham-maa-la-tal-ha-tab

Translation:
"And his wife too, the carrier of firewood" – 4

فِىْ جِيْدِهَا حَبْلٌ مِّنْ مَّسَدٍ 5

Transliteration:
Fee-jee-di-haa-hab-lum-mim-ma-sadh

Translation:
"Around her neck shall be a rope of twisted fibre" – 5

Chapter 112: Surah Al-Ikhlaas (The Sincerity of Purity)
4 Verses – 15 Words – 47 Letters

بِسْمِ اللهِ الرَّحْمٰنِ الرَّحِيْمِ

Transliteration:
Bis-mil-laa-hir Rahmaa-nir Raheem

Translation:
"In the name of Allah the most affectionate, the most merciful"

قُلْ هُوَ اللهُ اَحَدٌ ج 1

Transliteration:
Kul-hu-wal-laa-hu-ahad

Translation:
"Say, he Allah is one" – 1

اَللهُ الصَّمَدُ ج 2

Transliteration:
Allah-huss-sa-madh

Translation:
"Allah is independent from every need" – 2

لَمْ يَلِدْ وَلَمْ يُوْلَدْ لا 3

Transliteration:
Lam-ya-lidh-wa-lam-yu-ladh

Translation:
"He begot none, nor was he begotten (from anyone)"
– 3

وَلَمْ يَكُنْ لَّهٗ كُفُوًا اَحَدٌ ۴

Transliteration:
Wa-lam-ya-kul-lahu-ku-fu-wan-ahad

Translation:
"And there is none equal to him" – 4

Chapter 113: Surah Al-Falaq (The Daybreak)
5 Verses – 23 Words – 74 Letters

بِسْمِ اللهِ الرَّحْمٰنِ الرَّحِيْمِ

Transliteration:
Bis-mil-laa-hir Rahmaa-nir Raheem

Translation:
"In the name of Allah the most affectionate, the most merciful"

قُلْ اَعُوْذُ بِرَبِّ الْفَلَقِ ١

Transliteration:
Kul-a-oozu-bi-rab-bil-fa-laq

Translation:
"Say, I see refuge with the Lord of the day break" – 1

مِنْ شَرِّ مَا خَلَقَ ٢

Transliteration:
Min-shar-ri-maa-kha-laq

Translation:
"From the mischief of all creatures created by him" –
2

وَمِنْ شَرِّ غَاسِقٍ اِذَا وَقَبَ ٣

Transliteration:
Wa-min-shar-ri-ghaa-si-qin-izaa-waqab

"And from the evil of the darkness when it sets in" – 3

وَمِنْ شَرِّ النَّفّٰثٰتِ فِى الْعُقَدِ ٤

Transliteration:
Wa-min-shar-rin-naf-faa-saa-ti-fil-uqadh

Translation:
"And from the evil of those women who blow on the knots" – 4

وَمِنْ شَرِّ حَاسِدٍ اِذَا حَسَدَ ٥

Transliteration:
Wa-min-shar-ri-haa-si-din-izaa-ha-sadh

Translation:
"And from the evil of the envier when he envies (me)" – 5

Chapter 114: Surah An-Naas (The Mankind)
6 Verses – 20 Words – 79 Letters

بِسْمِ اللّٰهِ الرَّحْمٰنِ الرَّحِيْم

Transliteration:

Bism-illaa-hir Rahmaa-nir Raheem

Translation:

"In the name of Allah the most affectionate, the most merciful"

قُلْ اَعُوْذُ بِرَبِّ النَّاسِ ١

Transliteration:

Kul-a-oozu-bi-rab-bin-naas

Translation:

"Say (Oh Muhammad) I seek refuge with the Lord of mankind" – 1

مَلِكِ النَّاسِ ٢

Transliteration:

Ma-li-kin-naas

Translation:

"The king of mankind" – 2

اِلٰهِ النَّاسِ ٣

Transliteration:

Ilaa-hin-naas

مِنْ شَرِّ الْوَسْوَاسِ ۙ الْخَنَّاسِ 4

Transliteration:

Min-shar-ril-wass-waa-sil-khan-naas

Translation:

"From the evil of him who whispers evil designs in the hearts and slinks away" -4

الَّذِىْ يُوَسْوِسُ فِيْ صُدُوْرِ النَّاسِ ۙ 5

Transliteration:

Al-la-zee-yu-wass-wi-su-fee-su-duoor-rin-naas

Translation:

"Those who whisper in the hearts of mankind" – 5

مِنَ الْجِنَّةِ وَالنَّاسِ 6

Transliteration:

Mi-nal-jinn-na-ti-wan-naas

Translation:

"From among jinn and mankind" – 6

Dua for when waking up

اَلْحَمْدُ لِلّٰهِ الَّذِيْ أَحْيَانَا بَعْدَ مَا أَمَاتَنَا وَإِلَيْهِ النُّشُوْرُ

Transliteration:

Al-ham-du-lil-laa-hil-lazee-ah-yaa-naa-ba-da-maa-amaa-ta-naa-wa-ilay-hin-nu-shoor.

Translation:

"Praise is to Allah Who gives us life after He has caused us to die and to Him is the return."

Dua for when getting dressed

اَلْحَمْدُ لِلّٰهِ الَّذِيْ كَسَانِي هَذَا الثَّوْبَ وَرَزَقَنِيْهِ مِنْ غَيْرِ حَوْلٍ مِنِّي وَلَا قُوَّةٍ

Transliteration:

Al-hamdu-lil-laa-hil-lazee-kasaa-nee-ha-zath-thaw-ba-wa-ra-zaqa-nee-min- ghay-ree-haw-lim-min-nee-wa-laa-kuw-watin

Transliteration:

"Praise is to Allah Who has clothed me with this (garment) and provided it for me, though I was powerless myself and incapable."

NOTE: The sunnah is to put your clothes on, starting from the right. When taking off garments, one should start to take them off from the left. The same is true when putting on shoes. One should put the right shoe in first, then left. When taking footwear off, you should take the left off first, then the right.

Dua for entering washroom

اَللّٰهُمَّ إِنِّي أَعُوْذُ بِكَ مِنَ الْخُبْثِ وَالْخَبَائِثِ

Transliteration:

Allaa-hum-ma-in-nee-auzu-bika-mi-nal-khu-bthi-wal-kha-baaith

Translation:
"Oh Allah , I seek protection in You from the male and female unclean spirits."

Dua for leaving washroom

غُفْرَانَكَ الْحَمْدُ لِلّٰهِ الَّذِيْ أَذْهَبَ عَنِّي الْأَذٰى وَعَافَانِيْ

Transliteration:
Ghuf-ra-naka-al-ham-du-lil-la-hil-lazi-azhaba-an-nil-aza-wa-aa-faa-nee

Translation:
"(O Allah) I seek forgiveness and pardon from You, all Praise be to Allah, who has taken away from me discomfort and granted me relief."

Dua to read during Wudu (Ablution)

اَللّٰهُمَّ اجْعَلْنِيْ مِنَ التَّوَّابِيْنَ وَاجْعَلْنِيْ مِنَ الْمُتَطَهِّرِيْنَ

Transliteration:
Alla-hum-maj-alni-minat-taw-wab-ina-waj-al-ni-mi-nal-muta-tah-hirin

Translation:
"Oh Allah, make me *among those who turn to You in repentance, and make me among those who are purified.*"

NOTE: This dua can also be read when Wudu (ablution) is completed

Dua for leaving the house

بِسْمِ اللهِ تَوَكَّلْتُ عَلَى اللهِ وَلَا حَوْلَ وَلَا قُوَّةَ إِلَّا بِاللهِ

Transliteration:
Bis-mil-laahi-tawak-kaltu-al-alla-ahi-wa-laa-haw-la-wa-la-quw-wata-illaa-bil-laah

Translation:
"In the Name of Allah, I have placed my trust in Allah, there is no might and no power except by Allah."

Dua for when setting off on a journey

سُبْحَانَ الَّذِيْ سَخَّرَ لَنَا هَذَا

وَمَا كُنَّا لَهُ مُقْرِنِيْنَ وَإِنَّا إِلَى رَبِّنَا لَمُنْقَلِبُوْنَ

Transliteration:
Sub-ḥaan-alla-zhee-sakh-kha-ra-la-naa-ha-zha
wa-maa-kun-naa-la-hu-muq-ri-neena-
wa-in-naa-ilaa-rab-binaa-la-mun-qa-liboon

Translation:
"Glory to him who has brought this (vehicle) under our control, though we were unable to control it (ourselves), and indeed, too our Lord we will surely return."

Dua for entering the house

بِسْمِ اللهِ وَلَجْنَا وَبِسْمِ اللهِ خَرَجْنَا وَعَلَى رَبِّنَا تَوَكَّلْنَا

Transliteration:
Bis-mil-lahi-wa-laj-na-wabis-mil-lahi-kha-rajna-
wa-ala-rab-bina ta-wak-kal-na

Translation:
"In the name of Allah we enter, and In the name of Allah we leave, and upon our lord we place our trust"

Dua for entering the Masjid (Mosque)

أَعُوذُ بِاللهِ الْعَظِيمِ وَبِوَجْهِهِ الْكَرِيمِ وَسُلْطَانِهِ الْقَدِيمِ مِنَ الشَّيْطَانِ الرَّجِيمِ

Transliteration:

A-uzhu-bil-laa-hil-azhu-weem-wa-bi-waj-hi-hil-kareem-wa-sultaa-ni-hil-qa-deemi-min-ash-shay-taanir-ra-jeem

Translation:

"I seek refuge in Almighty Allah, by His noble face, by His primordial power, from Satan the outcast."

بِسْمِ اللهِ وَالصَّلَاةُ وَالسَّلَامُ عَلَى رَسُولِ اللهِ

Transliteration:

Bis-mil-laahi-wass-sa-laatu-wass-sa-laamu-ala-rasool-ilaah

Translation:

"In the Name of Allah, and salutations and peace be upon the Messenger of Allah (peace be upon him)."

اَللّٰهُمَّ افْتَحْ لِي أَبْوَابَ رَحْمَتِكَ

Transliteration:

Alla-hum-maf-tah-lee-ab-waa-ba-rahma-tika

Transliteration:

"Oh Allah, open before me the doors of Your mercy."

NOTE: This dua is in three parts which I have broken down to make it easier for the audience to read. When entering the Masjid (Mosque) one should step in the right foot.

Dua when leaving the Masjid (Mosque)

اَللّٰهُمَّ إِنِّي أَسْأَلُكَ مِنْ فَضْلِكَ وَرَحْمَتِكَ

Transliteration:

Alla-hum-ma-in-nee-as-aluka-min-fad-lika-wa-rahma-tika

Translation:

"Oh Allah indeed I ask of you for your virtue (bounty) and your mercy."

NOTE: When leaving the Masjid (Mosque) it is Sunnah to step out with your left foot.

Dua to say when overcome by weakness

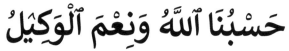

Transliteration:

Hass-bu-nalla-hu-wa-ni-mal-wa-keel

Translation:

"Sufficient for us is Allah, and he is the best disposer of affairs."

Dua for when something is becoming difficult

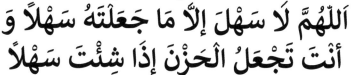

Transliteration:

Allaa-hum-ma-aa-sah-la-illa-ma-ja-al-tahu-sah-lan-wa-anta-taj-alul-haz-na-izha-shi-ta-sah-lan

Translation:

"Oh Allah, there is no ease other than what you make easy. If you please ease sorrow."

Dua for when it rains

اَللّٰهُمَّ صَيِّبًا نَّافِعًا

Translation:

Alla-hum-ma-sway-yi-ban-na-fi-an

Transliteration:
"Oh Allah, make it a beneficial rain."

Dua to read before eating

بِسْمِ اللهِ وَعَلَى بَرَكَةِ اللهِ

Transliteration:
Bis-mil-lahi-wa-ala-ba-ra-ka-til-lah

Translation:
"In the name of Allah and with the blessings of Allah I begin (eating)."

Dua to read when finished eating

اَلْحَمْدُ لِلّٰهِ الَّذِئْ اَطْعَمَنَا وَسَقَانَا وَجَعَلَنَا مُسْلِمِيْنَ

Transliteration:
Al-ham-du-lil-lahil-lazhi-ata-amana-wa-saqa-na-waj-alna-min-al-muslimeen

Translation:
"Praise be to Allah who has fed us and given us drink, and made us among the Muslims."

Dua for what the groom should say to his bride on the wedding night

بَا رَكَ اللهُ لِكُلِّ وَاحِدٍمِّنَّا فِيْ صَا حِبِهِ

Transliteration:
Ba-ra-kal-lahu-li-kuli-wa-hidim-min-na-fee-swaa-hi-bi-hi

Translation:

"May Allah bless each of us in our company."

NOTE: The groom should place his right hand on his brides forelock and read this dua (supplication).

Dua to read before sexual intercourse

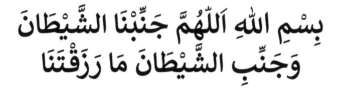

Transliteration:

Bis-mil-lahi-alla-hum-ma-jan-nib-nash-shay-tana
Wa-jan-ni-bish-shay-tana-ma-ra-zaq-tana

Translation:

"In the name of Allah. Oh Allah, keep the devil away from us and keep the devil away from that which you provide for us."

NOTE: The Prophet peace be upon him said if anyone reads this Dua and the married couple are destined a child, then Satan will never be able to harm that child.

Dua for when sneezing

اَلْحَمْدُ لِلّٰهِ

Transliteration:

Al-ḥam-du-lil-laah

Translation:

All praise is for Allah

Whoever hears the sneeze, should say:

Transliteration:
Yar-ha-mu-kal-laah

Translation:
"May Allah have mercy upon you."

NOTE: This is the response for if a male sneezes. If a female sneezes, then the respondents should read the Dua below.

Transliteration:
yar-ha-mu-kil-llaah

Translation:
"May Allah have mercy upon you."

NOTE: Once those who heard the sneeze have read the above Dua's. The person who sneezed then read the Dua below as a final response.

يَهْدِيكُمُ اللّهُ وَيُصْلِحُ بَالَكُمْ

Transliteration:
Yah-dee-kum-ul-laahu-wa-yus-lih-baa-lakum

Translation:
"May Allah guide you and rectify your condition"

Dua to read when burdened by debt

اَللّٰهُمَّ اكْفِنِيْ بِحَلَالِكَ عَنْ حَرَامِكَ
وَأَغْنِنِيْ بِفَضْلِكَ عَمَّنْ سِوَاكَ

..

Transliteration:
Alla-hum-mak-fi-nee-bi-ha-la-lika-an-ha-ra-mika-wa-agh-
ninee-bi-fad-lika-am-man-si-waka

Translation:
*"Oh Allah! Grant me enough of what You make lawful so
that I may dispense with what You make unlawful, and
enable me by Your Grace to dispense with all but You."*

Dua when placing the deceased into the grave

Transliteration:
Bis-mil-lahi-wa-ala-mil-lati-rasul-lil-laah

Translation:
*"In the name of Allah, and with Allah's help, and upon the
religion of Allah's messenger (peace be upon him)."*

Dua for when going to sleep

Transliteration:
Allaa-hum-ma-bis-mika-amu-tu-wa-ahyaa

Translation:
"Oh Allah in your name, I die and I live"

Closing Statement

All praise be to Allah, the Most High, the Most Gracious, and the Most Merciful. Peace and salutations upon the blessing of all creations, the final messenger, Prophet Muhammad, peace be upon him.

In the profound and enriching journey through the chapters of this book, we have traversed the intricate landscapes of Islamic wisdom, unraveling the profound teachings embedded within the pillars of our faith. These pillars, pillars of strength and guidance, have been our steadfast companions, leading us through the declaration of faith in Shahada, the disciplined and sacred act of Salah, the noble duty of Zakat, the self-restraint observed during Sawm, and the pilgrimage of Hajj. Beyond being mere rituals, they are gateways, gateways to a profound connection with the divine, guiding us towards a life of profound compassion, unwavering devotion, and a purposeful existence.

Each chapter has been a tapestry woven with threads of wisdom, drawing inspiration from the radiant life of Prophet Muhammad (peace be upon him), the steadfast companions, and the noble Imams. These teachings have not only revealed the external facets of the pillars but have also delved deep into the spiritual dimensions, resonating within the very core of Islam.

As we bid a fond farewell to the pages of this book, let us carry forward the profound lessons learned. This journey is not a conclusion; rather, it is a threshold towards a deeper understanding of spirituality within Islam. Beyond the confines of rules and rituals, we find the echoes of a spiritual resonance, beckoning us towards a connection that transcends the ordinary, unveiling the sublime nature of our faith.

Recognising the possibility of imperfections, your invaluable feedback is earnestly sought for the refinement of future editions. Kindly extend your thoughts for corrections at your earliest convenience. You may contact us on:

info@mjrpublishing.com

Or you can message us on Facebook/Instagram - @mjrpublishing

This book, transcending its role as a mere repository of knowledge, stands as a catalyst for spiritual ascent. May the teachings encapsulated within these pages be not just the end but the foundation for a profound inward journey. Let this be a pilgrimage towards a closer proximity to the divine, where each step is marked by an unwavering commitment to compassion, love, and understanding.

My heartfelt gratitude extends to Hafiz Mufti Maruf Ahmed and Hafiz Mawlana Abdul Wasi Arif for their tireless efforts in editing and revising this book. Their dedication has been pivotal in shaping this narrative.

May your pursuit of spiritual enlightenment be adorned with the grace of Allah. As you continue to traverse the depths of faith, spirituality, and the resplendent beauty of Islam, may Allah's guidance and blessings accompany each step on this sacred path.

At your service, your brother in faith.

Mohammed J. Rahman

Printed in Poland
by Amazon Fulfillment
Poland Sp. z o.o., Wrocław

33112385R00154